THE SMARTER PRESCHOOLER

Unlocking Your Child's Intellectual Potential

Renee Mosiman, M.A.
Mike Mosiman

BRIGHTER INSIGHTS
Mesa, Arizona

ISBN: 978-0-9816426-5-9

Editing by Elizabeth Zack and Sue Ducharme
Index by Diana Witt
Cover design by 1106 Design LLC
Design and composition by John Reinhardt Book Design

Printed In The United States Of America

To Our Sons,
Luke and Mark

Contents

Introduction

A CHILD'S FIRST YEARS are filled with play and exploration. For a little one, this is a time of innocence, one of freedom and discovery. Parents are filled with boundless joy over their newest family addition. In the middle of the second year, there is often a change. Parents change. Their minds become troubled. They begin to worry: "Am I doing enough to develop my child's intellect? What more can I do? Should I send my son or daughter to preschool?" In the recent past, preschool years were not filled with such parental concerns; the unstructured time a child enjoyed with parents during the toddler years continued through the preschool years until the youngster was ready to begin elementary school. Why the change?

Many Americans now place greater value on the intellect than in the past. Parents want their children to have every opportunity, and many believe their children will have fewer employment options if they leave the nest without a college degree. They want their kids to go a top-notch college, even if they themselves did not. But to gain admission, adolescents must be enrolled in a competitive high school. In order to get into the competitive high school, youngsters must attend a good junior high school. And of course to have even a remote chance of getting into the "good" junior high, a child must come from a fine elementary school. But the elementary school may prove elusive if parents did not find an elite preschool for their toddler!

Today children are spending more time in kindergarten; often free play and naps are sacrificed for reading and writing drills. In 1977, 27 percent of children attended full-day kindergarten; by 2001 that number was 60 percent.[1] Standardized tests have made their way into some kindergarten classrooms that evaluate their language arts, math, science, and social studies skills.[2] And in turn, these expectations create greater pressure for the academic achievement of preschool-aged children.

This sense of urgency has resulted in preschools, or "learning centers," popping up everywhere; they seem to be on every street corner. Many churches have even jumped on the bandwagon and now offer preschool programs. With the increase in academic pressure, preschool school days are getting longer, the number of days a week is increasing, and children are starting at younger ages.

Tutoring centers originally designed for school-aged children who needed extra attention have now developed programs for preschool children whose parents are hoping to give them an edge. Some parents even go as far as hiring private tutors, with the goal of providing their children with a smarter start.

In some larger cities the competition to get into the best preschool is so fierce that admission requirements include testing, interviews, and stellar recommendations. Some parents even pay thousands of dollars for preschool consultants to help their child get a coveted spot. For some preschools, long waiting lists are not uncommon. When we lived in Los Angeles, a work colleague said his son was on a waiting list for an elite preschool. The funny thing was, his bundle of pride and joy was still basking in his mother's womb. Plans were being made to put his child on the fast track, and he was not even born! This father-to-be then cautioned us not to delay making our own plans, even though we were newly married and had no children.

Product developers too are in high gear, creating the latest gadget to sharpen a youngster's intellect, promoted by marketing departments that promise your youngster will be Ivy League–bound if you just follow the instructions on the back of the package. Many of these products are based on scant research, if any, but feature a catchy name along with clever marketing. Often parents are being sold a bill of goods by being assured that the latest product will catapult their preschooler ahead of their peers intellectually. These promises come in all forms: videos, computer games, toys, and Web sites selling educational products.

We believe it is your responsibility as a parent to unlock your preschooler's intellectual potential, but we believe there is no shortcut or magic bullet. We urge you to create an intellectually *stimulating* environment, but not an intellectually *demanding* one. There is a tremendous difference.

Intellectually Demanding Environment

In an intellectually demanding environment, parents place too much emphasis on the intellect. This is unfortunate for the parent and bad for the child. For the parent, it creates extra stress and anxiety when the time should be spent enjoying a child's early years. These parents are overly concerned with milestones. Questions haunt them, such as "Why doesn't my child know all his letters?" "When should my child start reading?" and "Why can't my child write his or her name?" They fear their child will be left behind or not do as well as his or her peers.

In an intellectually demanding home, the child fares far worse than his or her peers. The time that should be reserved for freedom and exploration is supplanted by a time of anxiety. A child feels compelled to fulfill high parental expectations; this is fertile ground in which the seeds of unhappiness are sewn. In this environment, a child may believe that the parent's love is conditional—that in order to be loved, he or she must meet the lofty demands of the parent. Often this is not how the parent feels. In fact, many parents are doing what they believe is best for the youngster. Yet what is most relevant is not what the parent thinks but rather what the child perceives. If the child perceives a parent's love is conditional at a time the youngster needs support and encouragement, it can be devastating.

One indication of an intellectually demanding environment is one in which a child spends too much time running from one activity to the next. Spanish class, art class, and music class may be great for a youngster, but not in the same afternoon. In general, too much formal instruction time replaces free play or interacting with parents or friends.

Another characteristic is when a child is confronted with activities before he or she is developmentally ready for them. If a child is pressured to perform beyond his or her developmental level—i.e., to understand letter sounds too early or to write before he or she possesses the fine motor skills—it can damage or destroy a child's eagerness to learn, as well as his or her self-esteem.

Intellectually Stimulating Environment

On the other hand, an intellectually stimulating environment is child-focused and physically and verbally engaging, as well as emotionally supportive. Instead of focusing on a child primarily as a budding intellect, such an environment fosters a holistic view of a child. And rather than racing to the next milestone, the parent realizes every child is unique and develops at his or her own pace. Each child has special gifts, and it is the parent's job to cultivate a child's talents and strengthen his or her weaknesses.

Parents who create an intellectually stimulating environment do not feel compelled to compare their child with his or her peers. The child is then less anxious because he or she feels loved unconditionally, regardless of his or her achievements. Such parents carefully select outside activities, yet they do not overly schedule the child. And since there are fewer time constraints, the youngster has more time to experience being a child. There is plenty of play time to enjoy toys, parents, and peers, as well as leisurely reading time. Of course most parents want their child to be smart; by creating a stimulating yet undemanding environment, such parents can be confident that they are doing the most to unlock a child's intellectual potential.

Just to be clear, as authors, experts, and parents, we endorse academic rigor, but not for the preschool-age child. Learning at this age should be experiential. In an intellectually stimulating environment, a preschooler's mind is best sharpened through age-appropriate enriching activities under the guidance of a loving parent.

And although we do recommend some classroom activities specifically designed for the young student, we recommend them in appropriate doses and at the right time: not long daily classes filled with busy work, but activities that incorporate learning through play. Choosing developmentally appropriate activities for your child will lay the groundwork for his or her intellectual achievements by creating curiosity and a love for learning.

Creating the Right Environment

What you do in the early years will set precedents for your child for years to come. We wrote this book to help you create the best intellectually stimulating environment for your child. While there are many books about the cognitive development of infants and toddlers, fewer address children ages three to six, when the brain is going through tremendous changes; its capabilities greatly increase as the brain creates new connections and makes those existing more efficient. Growth and optimization of the preschooler's brain makes learning easier in the future. By following the methods and philosophy of this book, you will get your child off to a smarter start.

In a clear and accessible format, this book presents the latest quality research on developing a child's intellectual abilities. Then, based on co-author Renee's Masters of Counseling Psychology in Marriage and Family Therapy and her work with children in a clinical setting, combined with our first-hand knowledge from raising two children, we show you how to incorporate proven techniques into your daily routines.

Specifically, we will teach you how to develop the following capacities in your child:

- Critical thinking
- Problem solving
- General knowledge
- Pre-reading/reading skills
- Vocabulary
- Oral expression

- Oral comprehension
- Math skills
- Spatial ability
- Curiosity
- Creativity
- Love of learning

Following our approach, you will foster curiosity and a passion for learning in your child. You will train your preschooler to think analytically and develop problem-solving skills that will be valuable for a lifetime. You will improve communication with your child and build a stronger relationship with him or her. In turn, your youngster will respond with trust and curiosity and become a more emotionally healthy child.

To parents of children with developmental disabilities, please realize that our book is not meant as a substitute for professional help. And if you suspect your child may be outside the normal range of development, contact your pediatrician.

That said, we believe every child can benefit from our approach, whether a genius or more challenged, whether the youngster is enrolled in preschool or not.

—RENEE MOSIMAN and MIKE MOSIMAN, *November 2008*

Intelligence:
What Is It?

WHAT DO WE MEAN when we say someone is "intelligent"? Are we referring to someone who excels in academics? Has a great deal of general knowledge? Possesses a fantastic memory? Is well-spoken? Ask ten people, and you will likely get ten different answers.

Webster's Unabridged defines intelligence as the "capacity for learning, reasoning, understanding, and similar forms of mental activity; aptitude in grasping truths, relationships, facts, meanings, etc."[1] The majority of clinical experts agree intelligence includes "verbal ability, problem-solving skills, and the ability to learn from and adapt to the experiences of everyday life."[2]

Measuring Intelligence

The most widely accepted way to measure intelligence is the IQ test. In 1905, Frenchmen Alfred Binet and Theodore Simon were charged by the French Minister of Public Instruction to develop a test to determine if a child should be placed in special classes due to retardation.[3] They created the 1905 scale that consisted of thirty questions that tested a child's comprehension, memory, and reasoning. By 1908, Binet devised the concept of mental age that compared a child to his or her peers.[4] For example, he would identify a six-year-old who had the cognitive functioning of an eight-year-old as having a mental age of eight. William Stern built upon Binet's work by conceiving the intelligence quotient, or IQ, which

Number of Scores

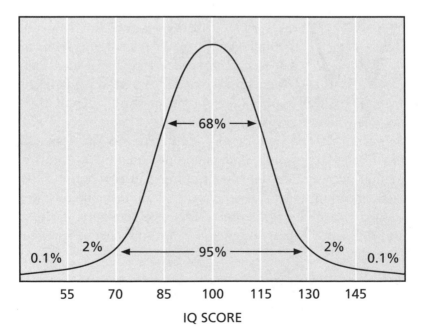

IQ SCORE

was derived by dividing a person's mental age by their actual age, then multiplying by 100.[5]

Since that time, IQ tests have evolved substantially. Today's scores are derived in comparison to one's peers and then normally distributed. This means the results form a bell curve, with most people having scores concentrated in the middle, around 100, while fewer individuals have extremely low or high scores.[6] (See Bell Curve Figure.)

Today the two IQ tests most widely used for preschool aged children are the Stanford-Binet Version 5 (SB5) and The Wechsler Preschool Primary Scale of Intelligence (WPPSI-III). The SB5 is used for ages two through eighty-five.[7] The examiner starts with questions based upon the chronological age of the person being tested; the accuracy of the answers determines which questions to ask next. The SB5 consists of five factors, and each contains a Verbal and Nonverbal section. They are:

- Fluid Reasoning: Object series and analogies
- Knowledge: General information and vocabulary
- Quantitative Reasoning: Problem solving
- Visual-Spatial Processing: Patterns and spatial orientation
- Working Memory: Storing and manipulating data

The test provides three IQ scales: a Verbal IQ, a Nonverbal IQ, and a combined Full Scale IQ.

The WPPSI-III is designed specifically for ages two and one-half through seven. Like the SB5, the WPPSI-III contains two sections: a Verbal scale, and a Nonverbal or Performance scale; the results of both are combined for a Full Scale IQ score. The two sections have a total of fourteen subtests: seven in Verbal and seven in Performance.

The seven Verbal subtests are:

- Vocabulary: Give word definitions
- Similarities: Make verbal analogies
- Information: Answer questions about common object and events
- Comprehension: Describe consequences of events
- Word Reasoning: Identify common objects based upon description
- Receptive Vocabulary: Identify one of four pictures based upon description
- Picture Naming: Name pictures shown

The seven Performance subtests are:

- Picture Completion: Identify what is missing from a picture
- Coding: Pair shapes
- Block Design: Reproduce patterns
- Matrix Reasoning: Identify missing object from a group
- Symbol Search: Identify specified symbol in group
- Object Assembly: Build puzzle
- Picture Concepts: Identify what is common between pictures[8]

Why Test Your Child's IQ?

Do we think you should immediately run out to have your child's IQ tested? No. Instead, IQ should be appropriately used to identify either gifted children or those with special needs. For example, if you find that your preschool-age child is not meeting normal milestones, a pediatrician may make a referral to a developmental specialist, who may use an IQ test to determine if there are cognitive problems prohibiting the child's development. On the other hand, if your child is gifted, there are programs for which your son or daughter would qualify based upon the testing results. But such programs generally start in elementary school, not at the preschool level.

A second useful role for IQ tests is for researchers to either validate a method or to test a hypothesis. For example, researchers may test an individual's IQ before and after an experiment to determine if there was an increase in cognitive abilities. Or they may test IQ to look for a correlation between intelligence and another variable, whether the amount of reading or television-watching or hours spent in preschool.

But if you test your child's IQ out of curiosity, you may make this number part of his or her identity—and this can be harmful. You may create expectations for your youngster based upon an IQ number. This, in turn, can impact a youngster's self-worth. A child may feel inadequate if he or she never reaches the goals your have set, and your youngster may carry this damaged self-image into his or her adult life.

Presumptions founded upon IQ scores alone can also shape a child's behavior. Parents may permit behavior that may have otherwise not have been tolerated, due to either a high or low perceived intellect. For example, a mom or dad may excuse a youngster's lack of effort by reasoning that the child with a lower IQ has a lack of aptitude. Parents who have low expectations based upon an intelligence test might not sufficiently challenge a child to reach his or her full potential. On the other hand, parents may excuse poor behavior in a bright child because they believe they need not worry about their youngster getting into trouble.

Armed with the knowledge of a child's intelligence quotient, a parent may create a one-dimensional child. For example, if you believe your child is not smart, you may be more inclined to direct him or her away from intellectual pursuits that you may otherwise have promoted. Or if you discover that your child is particularly gifted in math, you may overemphasize math and neglect the child's other areas of study.

If you have two kids, there could be double trouble. For instance, you may not resist the temptation to compare siblings to one another. You may encourage the child with the higher IQ to enroll in more advanced classes, while not suggesting such classes for the other—even though both may be capable.

Even when parents do not articulate a comparison, it may be on their mind for years. We personally know parents who had each of their three children's IQs tested at early ages. Twenty years later, the mom still knows the IQ of each child. And although she has never mentioned exact numbers, she has commented that she cannot understand why the child with the highest IQ isn't more successful. Ironically, the child with the highest IQ test score was the one who struggled the most through school. Although these children are now adults, the mom still expects more from her son with the higher IQ and less from her sons with the lower scores.

In general, IQ testing can also be a symptom of parents placing too much emphasis upon intelligence, while other qualities essential for future success, such as tenacity, are neglected. Also, the average person does not recognize that a few points difference in IQ points does not translate into a major difference in intellect.

Theories of Intelligence

Some psychologists have departed from the idea of determining an intelligence quotient and instead developed theories to conceptualize intelligence. They view intelligence through a more subjective lens. For example, Robert Sternberg developed the Triarchic Theory of Intelligence, in which there are three types of intelligence: Analytical, Creative, and Practical.[9] He defines Analytical Intelligence as the ability to reason and evaluate; these are people who often do well in school and on traditional IQ tests. Those who posses Creative Intelligence can solve new problems with novel ideas and may be inventors or artists. Finally, Sternberg says people who possess Practical Intelligence use "street smarts" to solve problems. They may not do as well in the classroom setting, but they do very well in other areas, such as sales or management.

Sternberg's contemporary Howard Gardner developed the Theory of Multiple Intelligence to describe different types of personal intelligences. Here they are, as well as potential career choices.

- Linguistic: Speaking and writing ability
  CAREERS: *Author, Lawyer, Speaker*

- Logical-Mathematical: Mathematical and logical operations ability
  CAREERS: *Engineer, Scientist, Mathematician*

- Musical: Musical talent
  CAREERS: *Composer, Singer, Pianist*

- Body-Kinesthetic: Gross or fine motor skills
  CAREERS: *Athlete, Ballerina, Surgeon*

- Spatial: Ability to manipulate objects in space
  CAREERS: *Engineer, Architect, Pilot*

- Interpersonal: Works well with others
  CAREERS: *Counselor, Minister, Teacher*

- Intrapersonal: Knows him or herself, or is self-reflective
  CAREERS: *Philosopher, Psychologist, Theologian*[10]

■ Naturalist: Adept at working in a natural environment
CAREERS: *Botanist, Forest Ranger, Landscaper*[11]

Unlike Stanford-Binet and Wechsler's theories, which are analytically supported, neither Gardner nor Sternberg's theories are supported by quantitative data.[12] Lacking empirical support does not necessarily make them invalid, but when you look at the lists of intelligences Gardener compiled, you find the types resemble personal characteristics. These qualities do not have less value than the intellect; in fact, they may well be more important for personal achievement or happiness. But this list of personal qualities tells little of the cognitive functioning of a person. We believe to identify athletic ability as intelligence, for instance, is not really justified.

What Factors Influence Intelligence?

Now that we have looked at the metrics of intelligence used today, one important question remains: What factors influence the intellect?

Here we turn to the familiar nature versus nurture argument. Although experts continue to debate the proportional influence of genetics versus environment on intelligence, all agree both contribute to a child's intelligence. Even Richard Herrnstien and Charles Murray, who argue the case for the genetic influence on intelligence, agree that about 40 percent of your smarts are a result of your environment.[13] And since we cannot alter a child's genetic code, the sure way to make your preschooler smarter is to take a multidimensional approach to enriching his or her environment. In the chapters that follow, we will show you how.

The Growing Mind:

Your Preschooler's Cognitive Development

B EFORE WE OFFER WAYS to make your child smarter, you must be convinced that as a parent, you can make a difference—that what you do or don't do has an impact on the development of your youngster's mind. Fortunately, decades of neurological research and developmental psychology can provide insights into how the young mind works.

The Brain, Up Close

To understand the changes occurring in your young child's brain, let's start with a look at the brain's building block: the neuron. The brain contains 100 billion of these cells, the neurons, that transmit and receive chemical messages to one another across a space called the "synaptic gap." The neuron itself consists of an axon, which transmits chemical messages, and the dendrite, which receives messages. (See Neuron Figure.)

Both the neuron and the axon become larger when stimulated by the environment; the dendrite grows more branches, and the axon increases in length. With additional dendrite branches, not only can more data be stored, but the greater number of paths also results in easier access to and retrieval of information. Those branches that are stimulated regularly become stronger, while those not used wither and die. And the more often the brain receives the same stimulation, the more permanent, or hard-wired, the information becomes. A good analogy is a path in a forest or meadow: the heavier the traffic, the more distinct the trail becomes. A skill that becomes hardwired is riding a bicycle. Once you learn how to ride a bike, you can jump on your bike years later without having to relearn the skill.

Another way the brain increases its capability is by eliminating those branches that are not used via a process called

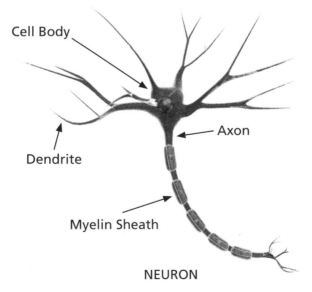

NEURON

"pruning." Just as superfluous branches of a tree are trimmed, the brain removes unneeded dendrites, thereby making the remaining connections more efficient. Here the old adage "use it or lose it" applies.

A final way the brain matures is by coating the axon with a fatty substance called a "myelin sheath." This acts as insulation so the chemical messages are carried more efficiently, much as the insulation around a wire ensures that electricity is conducted. An increase in myelin is the primary factor in the weight gain of the brain in the early years of life.

Malleable Matter

Prior to the 1960s, researchers believed the brain was immutable, its capabilities fixed from birth, regardless of the amount and type of stimulation. That perception changed as a result of groundbreaking research by Marian Diamond and her colleagues at the University of California at Berkeley.[1] The Berkeley team created two different environments for baby rats: one offered a variety of toys—an enriched environment—and the other had no toys, creating an impoverished environment. After mature growth, the rat's abilities were tested, and the brains from the rats in each of the two environments were compared. The rats that matured in a stimulating environment had bigger brains and could find their way through mazes for a food reward more quickly.[2] They were smarter rats.

Interestingly, observation alone is ineffective to develop the brain; there must be active engagement.[3] For example, rats that simply watched other rats in an enriched environment did not show much increase in brain size over those rats who grew in a deprived environment. Seeing may be believing, but observation alone does little to increase brain matter.

In the end, many scientists believe that "Early experiences determine which neurons are to be used and which are to die, and consequently, whether the child will be brilliant or dull, confident or fearful, articulate or tongue-tied."[4]

Plasticity

Learning comes more easily to the youthful brain. At this time, the brain has more than enough branching dendrites and is more active than an adult brain, as shown by its glucose consumption, which peaks during a child's preschool years.[5] A child's brain is biologically programmed to easily absorb new information; neurobiologists refer to the ability to change as being plastic.

In most cases, the brain retains some plasticity over the course of a lifetime, or else you could never learn anything new. But for optimal development, proper enrichment must occur during a specific timeframe, which is termed the critical period. Sight and language are two such abilities that have a distinct critical period. In the 1960s, Harvard researchers David Hubel and Torsten Wiesel showed that if a kitten's eye was sewn shut shortly after birth, eyesight could never be restored because the vision had been obstructed during the critical period of development.[6] The neural pathways that existed for sight had been pruned away due to disuse and could not be regenerated. Like kittens, children have a critical period for vision, but the critical time span lasts much longer. Children who have worn a patch during the critical period for vision have developed impaired sight.

The existence of a critical period for language development has also been demonstrated in a few rare cases in which a young child was separated from all human contact and survived in the wild, or in severe cases of child abuse.[7] These isolated children had no verbal interaction with other people and thus were unable to fully regain speech abilities in adolescent or adulthood.

Milestones

The brain is pre-programmed to reach developmental milestones in approximately the same order and rate. A newborn's brain is prepared for basic operations such as regulating heartbeat, breathing, and body temperature, as well as the senses of smell, taste, and touch. Vision and hearing are more primitive at birth, and full maturation of these senses occurs later. For example, a newborn perceives an object twenty feet away as if it were six hundred feet in the distance.[8] By the end of the first year, the child's vision is about 20/20. However, other visual capabilities, such as depth perception, continue to develop after the first year. Size constancy, which is the ability to comprehend that an object stays the same size whether it is nearer or farther in distance, also continues to develop until age ten.

Hearing too improves steadily through childhood. An infant's ability to hear different frequencies consistently improves and is almost fully developed by six months, while the ability to distinguish sounds among a noisy background does not fully mature until around age ten. Hearing capacities continue to be fined-tuned into puberty.[9]

Gross motor skills, which use large muscles, and fine motor skills, which require more precise movements such as finger dexterity, develop rapidly in young children. At birth, infants have no appreciable control of their arms or legs. Yet most children are walking by twelve or thirteen months and by three years running, hopping, and jumping.[10] Also, at birth, infants have next to no control of fine motor skills, although soon a youngster will grasp and hold objects.[11] All these improvements are a result of rapid cellular changes in the brain.

As a child enters the preschool years, changes continue in the brain, although not as rapidly. Gross motor skills continue to improve: a preschooler no longer toddles but is able to run and climb with ease. Building blocks and jigsaw puzzles become easier to manage as fine motor skills also become refined.

Cognitive changes also occur. A child's short-term memory increases through the preschool years. At age two, a child can remember two digits; by the time he or she is seven, this number increases to five digits.[12] Language skills improve as children learn more words, and their sentences become longer and more complex. A preschooler's attention span also increases significantly. The toddler's attention wanders easily, shifting from one object or activity to another, while the preschooler is able to stay on task longer.

Piaget

Famous Swiss psychologist Jean Piaget formulated a cognitive development theory to describe how a child's thinking evolves. Here's a brief look at all four of his stages, so you can understand what is normal in your preschooler's cognitive development and not place unrealistic expectations on children before they are ready. Piaget's four stages are:

- Sensorimotor Stage (ages 0–2)
- Preoperational Stage (ages 2–7)
- Concrete Operation Stage (ages 7–11)
- Formal Operation Stage (ages 11–15)[13]

According to his theory, children start life in the sensorimotor stage: They coordinate their senses and physical actions to understand the world.[14] For example, an infant in a high chair learns cause and effect by dropping his or her food on the floor and then observes what happens, often much to the chagrin of an on-looking parent. Early in this stage, infant believes an object no longer exists when it disappears from his or her sight. By the end of the sensorimotor stage, however, the child realizes that an out-of-sight object is still there. Piaget termed this concept "object permanency."

Key to Piaget's stages are the ideas of operations, which he defines as reversible mental exercises.[15] The second stage, called preoperational, is when children can perform some basic, but flawed, reasoning. He terms this stage as preoperational because a child is unable to perform more complicated exercises that use abstract symbols, such as mathematical symbols to add or subtract. At this stage they do, however, use some crude representations, such as a stick figure that represents their dad. During the preoperational stage children also begin pretend play. For example, a young child may imitate mommy when she feeds her stuffed animals (the children) by placing crayons (pretzels) in front of them for dinner. Through play, children learn to adjust to the world around them.[16]

Another characteristic of this preoperational stage is a self-centered worldview; children can only see the world from their perspective.[17] Ask your four-year-old over the phone about a picture he or she drew, and you will likely get the response, "See! Here it is." The child does not understand you cannot see what he or she sees if you are not there too. Piaget and psychologist Barbel Inhelder devised an experiment to show a child's lack of perspective. A child was seated in a position with a view different than the doll's. When the child was shown a series of pictures and asked which would represent the view the doll would see, he or she would select the picture of what he or she saw, rather than one from the doll's vantage point.

In the latter part of the preoperational stage, which is between four and seven years old, children gain some primitive reasoning skills. But most of what a child knows is through intuition, rather than rational thinking. In a classic experiment, Piaget shows children at this age are not able to fully reason. He filled two identical wide beakers with equal amounts of liquid. A third container had the same volume as the first two but a different shape; it was tall and thin. A child in the preoperative stage consistently believes the tall, thin beaker contains more liquid. Even when the youngster witnesses the liquid from the shorter, wider beaker being poured into the tall, thin beaker, the child will think the tall, thin beaker contains more liquid.

During Piaget's concrete operational stage, which lasts from ages seven to eleven, a youngster can perform mental exercises on real objects.[18] For example, at this stage a child is better able to classify and sort items by their unique characteristics, such as by size or shape. A child also understands a transitive relationship between objects. For instance, if ball one is bigger than ball two, and ball two is bigger than ball three, then the youngster understands that ball one is bigger than ball three. And the child can now understand the conservation task that he or she struggled with at the preoperational stage. A youngster knows that pouring a liquid from a tall, thin beaker into a short, stout container does not decrease the amount of liquid.

By the time a child is eleven, he or she enters Piaget's final stage of cognitive development, called the formal operational stage.[19] At this time, a youngster becomes capable of the abstract reasoning and thought required to devise plans, goals, and hypothetical thinking.

So, as you can see, a child goes through many changes throughout his or her preschool years. As the youngster matures, his or her brain develops, leading not only to new motor skills, but greater cognitive skills. By being aware of these changes, you can guide your child to make the most out of his or her natural abilities.

All in the Family:

The Impact of Familial Relationships on Intelligence

FAMILIES ARE CONSIDERED the fundamental building blocks of every society. And for good reason. Our immediate family shapes us in every way, especially during the formative preschool years. Sure, genetics play a role. But who we become in a large part is due to familial relationships. Our values, morals, and, to a large extent, even our personality and intellectual abilities are formed during our younger years by our families.

Family Structure

The family structure has a significant impact on the development of a young child—and that includes the intellect. A Phoenix-area elementary school teacher we know with fifteen years of experience told us she can consistently identify a child's family structure after spending the first week of school with the children. Based upon the social and academic performance of the students, she can tell who comes from a two-parent household versus those who live with a single parent. During the second week of the school year, she meets the children's parents at parent-teacher conferences and confirms her impression. She tells us she has yet to be wrong.

In an article titled "Family Structure and Children's Educational Outcomes," Donna Ginther from the University of Kansas and Robert Pollak from Washington University found that children raised outside traditional nuclear families had worse educational outcomes. The metrics included the youngsters' years of schooling, whether they graduated from high school, whether they attended college, and whether they graduated from college.[1] The researchers concluded that children from neither blended families nor single parent families perform as well on these metrics as those from "intact" families.

If you find yourself in a outside a traditional family structure, you can still do a good job parenting. The statistics indicate your child is at greater risk academically, but if you are aware of these risks, you can work to mitigate them. The most important thing you can do is to make sure you spend extra time with your child. If you are a single parent, your time is generally limited, so you may want to ask for help from close friends or relatives to relieve some of the burdens.

For single parents whose own parents are involved grandparents, there is also some encouraging news. A study from Cornell University found that children of single mothers who have a grandparent living with them can do as well academically as those in a traditional family.[2] Getting Grandpa or Grandma involved in a child's life may alleviate some of the problems inherent in a single-parent family. The extra help at home probably allows a single parent to spend more time with the kids than if one adult is saddled with all the responsibility for raising a child, running a household, and earning wages.

Even traditional families face challenges. Mom or Dad may work long hours or travel on business or both parents may choose to work, leaving less time available to spend with the children. And, sadly, sometimes even when family members live together, each person is doing his or her own thing. Dad may be reading a newspaper, Mom may be busy scrapbooking, Brother may be playing a computer game, and Sister may be watching her latest DVD. While we all need time to pursue individual interests, time should be reserved to do things as a family.

The Parent/Child Relationship

The Secure Attachment

From birth until about age three, a youngster establishes a bond, or attachment, to the mother. (We use "mother" here, as opposed to "father" or "parent," because nearly all the research examines the child's relationship with the mother.) This attachment is either secure or insecure. In the 1970s, psychologist Mary Ainsworth created a procedure called the "Strange Situation" to determine how the child is attached to the mother.[3] Ainsworth simply placed infants and their mothers in a new environment and observed how the children responded. Those children who had a secure attachment would explore the room, return to mom, and then resume exploration. For these children, mom was considered the "secure base," where they could return for emotional comfort, and then, confident again, continue on their own. When mom left the room, a securely attached child would mildly protest, then resume exploration. The child would reestablish the bond when she returned.

An insecure attachment was further categorized as either avoidant or resistant. Insecurely attached avoidant children would, as the name implies, avoid the mother in a new situation. These children would not interact with the mother when she was in the room; they were not distressed when she left; nor would they reconnect with her when mom returned. On the other hand, the insecurely attached resistant child would at first cling to the parent, then reject attention. He or she would cry loudly upon the mother's departure and not explore the room. When mom returned, the child would push her away.

Later, a third type category of insecurely attached children was added by other psychologists; they were identified as disorganized. These children might appear dazed, confused, or fearful in the new environment. The disorganized children might also express anger or hostility.

How is a baby's response in the Strange Situation relevant to your preschooler? As John Bowlby, the chief architect of attachment theory, stated, the early attachment children establish with their mothers is an indicator of future social and emotional behaviors and predicts how a "child in the age range of 4½ to 6 years will approach a new person and tackle a new task"[4] Additionally, over the past decades substantial research has been conducted to verify the benefits of a securely attached child in establishing and maintaining relationships. Those preschool children who have secure attachments:

- Are more confident
- Display greater curiosity
- Are more resourceful in novel situations
- Show greater leadership among their peers
- Are more interactive with their peers[5]

Research has also shown a correlation between the mother-child relationship and intelligence. Lisa Crandell and Peter Hobson from Tavistock Clinic in London, England, studied middle-class children between the ages of three and four.[6] The researchers determined whether children had a secure or insecure attachment to their mothers based upon a parental questionnaire and by observing parent-child interactions during free play. They tested the IQs of both the children and their mothers. The children who had a secure attachment to their mothers had IQs that were twelve points higher than children with an insecure attachment. The differences in IQ remained significant even when the mother's education, social economic status, and IQ were considered.

In a study titled "The Role of Home Literacy Practices in Preschool Children's Language and Emergent Literacy Skills," Joanne Roberts and her colleagues from the University of North Carolina followed seventy-two children from their first year up to kindergarten to determine how the frequency and manner in which mothers read to their children impacted their language and literary skills.[7] The researchers also rated the quality and quantity of the stimulation and support available to the child as scored by the Home Observation for Measurement of the Environment (HOME) Inventory. The HOME Inventory considers such factors as the available learning materials, the responsiveness of the parent, the exposure to language, and the variety of experiences for the child. The team found that while the child's literary exposure was important, the responsiveness and support of the home environment contributed to children's early language and literacy development over and above literacy practices. In other words, the relationship between a child and his or her mother matters most to literacy skills.

Likewise, Rebecca Fewell and Barabara Deutscher from

the University of Miami compared moms who had a more responsive maternal style to those who had a more direct style.[8] The researchers concluded that responsiveness contributed to a child's verbal IQ and reading level. On the other hand, a directive style was negatively correlated with both the child's verbal IQ and reading level. Other researchers also correlate a sensitive mother to a child's later math and academic achievements.[9]

Finally, Robert Pianta and Katrina Harbors from the University of Virginia found that interactions between kindergarten children and their mothers were predictors of academic achievement in elementary school.[10] The researchers evaluated both the mothers and children during problem-solving tasks to determine the nature of their relationship. The moms were rated on their emotional support, their ability to explain a task, and whether they encouraged their children's independence. At the same time, the children were rated on several points: their attitude and affection towards their moms; whether they were too reliant upon their moms to solve the tasks; how they followed their moms' instructions; and if they had healthy self-esteem. The kindergarten children who had better working relationships with their moms were stronger academically in elementary school.

Strikingly, the advantage to those children who had the better relationships with their mothers remained even when the influence of mom's education level was removed from consideration. This is significant because the mother's education is recognized as a robust predictor of academic success.[11]

Likewise, a team from the University of Minnesota followed children from birth through third grade and found, "Mothers' quality of instruction, parental involvement in school, and parental expectations have an effect on children's achievement *over and above* mother's education level, children's IQ, and children's previous achievement."[12] (Italics added.) The good news: By being attentive and spending time with a child, a less-educated mother can mitigate many of the advantages a more highly-educated parent has.

Creating a Secure Attachment

Researchers have extensively studied different parenting attributes and identified characteristics that are important in the development of a child. The maternal qualities that foster a secure attachment bond with an infant remain the same throughout a child's life. Obviously, the type of interaction will change as the child grows older. For example, you may respond to your crying infant by holding your baby, but your preschooler may need assistance doing a jigsaw puzzle instead of comfort.

One desirable parenting attribute is warmth, which may be demonstrated in several ways: verbally, physically, or in other expressive forms. Make sure to show you care by giving your child praise and encouragement. Not only what you say but how you speak to your youngster will make a difference in your child's attachment. Your child will respond better to patience and attentiveness.

Give plenty of accolades. Think of yourself as your child's personal cheerleader. A child never tires of being told he or she is doing a great job, and there are few better ways to build a child's healthy self-image than praise. When your youngster does something well, make sure it does not go unnoticed—give a compliment. By doing so, you build a child's sense of self worth. You let your child know that he or she matters. In turn, your youngster will be more confident in whatever he or she does. And your child will carry this confidence, developed in early childhood, into adulthood.

Social psychologist Carol Dweck from Columbia University has shown not all praise given to children is equal.[13] Interestingly, she found that students' perception of intelligence affects both their own personal motivation and performance. Dweck places people, based upon their perception of intelligence, into two categories: those who believe intelligence is fixed at birth, and those who feel it is malleable, so that with effort, a person can increase his or her intellectual abilities. Those who believed their intellect was fixed put forth less effort and had less academic success. In contrast, kids who thought they could boost their intellect through hard work did better and enjoyed learning more.

Dweck argues that the perception of either a fixed or malleable view of intelligence can be shaped. Those children whose intelligence was praised viewed their intellect as fixed, whereas those who received accolades for their effort perceived intellect as mutable. She suggests that rather than praising a child's intellect, you should praise his or her effort.

Rather than:
  You are so smart!
Try this:
  You did a great job coloring your picture!

In addition to verbal praise, physical expression is also meaningful. A pat on the back or kiss on the cheek are two examples. Other displays of affection that are neither verbal nor physical may include a wink or a smile. These are subtle but can be consistent reminders to your child that he or she matters. Do not wait for a grand event to show warmth—any time is the right time.

Mom should be sensitive and responsive. She should identify her child's cues and respond appropriately and consistently to the youngster's needs. For the very young, or infants, this is straightforward: the baby cries, and you provide food or change a diaper. With a preschool-age child, you need to be aware the child needs help and then provide the proper level of assistance. Give your child enough support to complete a task but to still be challenged. Let him or her maintain a sense of autonomy even though you are lending a hand. Your objective is to stay in what Lev Vygotsky, a contemporary developmental psychologist of Piaget's, called the "zone of proximal development": the ideal balance between a task that is too easy and one that is too difficult.[14] Your youngster's mind will develop best when stimulated incrementally. For example, if your child can do a 25-piece puzzle with ease, try a 50-piece puzzle. When the 50-piece is mastered, try 100 pieces.

On the other hand, if tasks are out of the proximal zone, or beyond your child's developmental level, your youngster will let you know—often in no uncertain terms. As parents, we purchased Hi Ho! Cherry-O to play with our two-and-a-half-year-old son. In this game, each player starts with a tree full of cherries and removes the number indicated by the spinner. The player who removes his or her fruit from the tree by placing them in their bucket first, wins. The game started out well, but after a few spins, he tossed his cherries. The game was clearly beyond his current ability level, so we put it away. A couple months later we revisited Hi Ho! Cherry-O; everyone had a great time.

And lastly, keep a positive attitude when working with your child. We know there are some days when being a parent is difficult, but try to remain patient. Remember they are not miniature adults, but children. They lack not only the physical and mental skills of adults, but also emotional maturity. Never resort to saying something that will demean or degrade your child. Berating a child is a sure way to break the spirit and to destroy a youngster's self-worth. This is especially true when scorn comes from the most trusted person in a child's life: the parent. If your youngster does something incorrectly, gently correct him or her or work together to find the solution:

> *No, honey, that letter is "b," not "d." I can see how you mixed them up, because they look similar but are reversed.*

> *I see that you are trying to put these pieces together, but it's not working. If we put them together like this, they may fit. Let's try it.*

Spend Lots of Time with Your Child

As a parent, you have probably discovered your youngster's demand for your time is insatiable. There is never enough of you to go around. Unfortunately, many believe quality time is a substitute for quantity time. This is not true. Your youngster needs *lots* of quality time. And what is quality time? We digested piles of studies that examined the parent/child relationship. What we found was surprisingly simple: Quality time is any time spent actively engaging with your child.

Quality time need not be glamorous, and it need not be exclusive. You may take your child to a special event to be sure, but the time you spend together may be as ordinary as a trip to the grocery store or a stroll around the neighborhood. A trip to the park, completing a puzzle, or playing catch in the backyard may be more rewarding and memorable than an expensive trip to an amusement park.

What about Dad?

Even though studies almost exclusively look at the mother/child relationship, those maternal qualities critical for the development of your child should also come from the father. Like mothers, dads need to actively engage their children in play by talking and interacting, not just passively observing.

Fathers can also add a new dimension to the parent/child

interaction. When they play with the kids, fathers tend to engage their children more physically, in more rough and tumble play.[15] In fact, much as the mother is often considered the primary caregiver, the father may be viewed as the primary playmate.

A friend of ours became a new father by adoption. He confessed that he did not know what to do with his little one when Mom left for her part time job, so he regularly placed his daughter behind the TV to watch the latest Baby Einstein video. We told him Dad can't get off that easily. Engage your daughter and play!

Siblings

For generations, much importance has been placed on children's birth order. In past eras, the firstborn likely inherited everything, and for the fortunate few, this could mean ruling a kingdom.

Recently, researchers have looked to find if there is anything behind the mythical importance of birth order. Norwegians Petter Kristensen and Tor Bjerkedal found older siblings had higher IQs, and each successive child had a lower IQ.[16] But they provided convincing evidence this was due to environmental factors, rather than genetic or biological, as had been previously postulated. Prior theories had hypothesized in utero conditions had caused the lower IQ scores—that subsequent pregnancies increased the number of antibodies present, and these were detrimental to brain development.

Kristensen and Bjerkedal studied 241,310 eighteen- and nineteen-year-old men who were drafted into the Norwegian military and looked for a correlation between the IQs of the men and their birth order. They grouped the men by birth order and compared their IQs. They found the birth order was inversely related to the men's IQ scores: Those who were second-born had a slightly lower IQ than those who were firstborns, and those who were a third child had slightly lower IQ scores than the second. But what was most compelling was that second-born men whose older sibling had died early in their childhood had IQs similar to those of the men who were firstborns. In these cases, the second child had effectively been raised with the environmental advantages of a firstborn. The study shows that the higher IQ of older children can thus be attributed to social factors, rather than a biological reason.

The researchers affirmed what we discovered as parents after our second son was born: The second child never has the same environment as the first. Before we were parents, we adopted the sentiment we heard from other parents, or society in general: "I don't know why little Johnny turned out like that—look at his older brother. He came from the *same* home and had the *same* opportunities." Clearly, genetics is a factor; everyone comes out of the womb as a unique person. However, *little Johnny did not have the same environment!* From the first breath he drew, little Johnny was competing with his older brother for Mom or Dad's attention. This was not the case for the firstborn child; it was all about him from day one. And does this affect the cognitive and emotional development of the younger child? Absolutely.

Often, too, there is a gradual change in parental attitude with the addition of each sibling. There is only one first time for anything, and raising children is no exception. As the eldest child, he or she is a novel experience for the parents. Parents generally put the most worry and effort into their first child; they want to be the best moms and dads they can possibly be. By the second or third child, the novelty wears off. Of course parents want to continue to do a good job, but everything need not be as "perfect" as the first time, so sometimes less effort goes into subsequent children.

It is a parent's responsibility to moderate the effects of being a second- or later-born child. For starters, make sure younger children have their own alone time with you. As we mentioned earlier, the firstborn had his or her time twenty-four hours a day, seven days a week, until the second birth. It is only fair that you *try* to give your younger child some of the same undivided attention. You can have time together when the older child is in classes, for example.

Also attempt to give the younger children similar opportunities: the same music classes, the same art classes, or the same playgroup times. Schedule carefully so that each child gets his or her own activities. One parent can watch one child while the other parent takes a child to class or playgroup. As parents, we were fortunate to have grandparents who were willing and able to watch big brother, but you may want to find a babysitter or swap childcare.

It is equally important to encourage each child to pursue his or interests—even when they have different talents. A family we know has a son who is an outstanding gymnast. His parents make tremendous sacrifices in hopes of developing a future Olympian. When his younger brother asked to play baseball, the parents said they would like to get the younger son involved in a team sport, but the older son's gymnastics are the priority. Even to a dispassionate observer, it is disturbing to know the younger son will spend his childhood in the shadow of his older sibling.

When you are together as a family, make sure the younger siblings are able to speak for themselves. Often an older child will want to help out and answer questions for the younger brother or sister, so make sure the smallest voice is heard. At dinnertime, listen to everyone's story of the day's events. Of course, the youngest sometimes needs a little help or prompting, but let that come from you rather than a helpful sibling. Discipline, too, is where an older child is more than willing to assist. As parents, our rule is unless the situation is life-threatening, the older is not to provide any help in the discipline department. Finally, reading time can be an opportunity for the little ones to shine. As older siblings learn to read, they take pride in reading to a younger brother or sister. This is fine, but give the little ones a chance. Let them "read" to the older siblings. Of course, they may not be reading at all, but you will be surprised how well they recall the stories as they page through the pictures.

Although it is easy and almost natural to do so, *never compare siblings with one another*. For example, a well-meaning parent may attempt to motivate a younger child by pointing out an older sibling's achievements. On the other hand, a parent may have unrealistically higher expectations for older siblings. But comparisons between siblings can be caustic in the long-run. Remember, all children are unique, develop at different rates, and have different talents. People learn in a variety of ways and may require many types of learning tools and techniques. Foster individual strengths, and each child will live up to his or her fullest potential.

With multiple children there is also a power differential between them. This too affects children's personality and emotional development. And this difference is typically maintained throughout childhood. The older sibling is not only physically bigger and stronger but knows more about everything. As parents, it is your responsibility to reduce the impact of this disparity on the younger child.

There are some advantages to not being first, however. Younger children learn from older children through instruction or by modeling the other children's behavior. Therefore, the younger siblings have the opportunity to be introduced to material sooner than their older siblings were. And while the younger kids learn, the older ones can benefit too by reinforcing what they already know. Not only is it an opportunity to build their minds, it also will create a stronger bond between the children. Siblings can contribute to one another's intellectual growth.

Another advantage of being the second, or third, child is that parents have more practice. When you practice a skill you become more proficient—and parenting is no different. Think of your first child as a test run, or a prototype version. After your first attempt, parenting is no longer unfamiliar territory. Hopefully you have compiled some "lessons learned" that you can apply to the subsequent siblings. Of course, children are never carbon copies of one another; each one rolls off the assembly line a unique model. So part of savvy parenting is to adapt your skills set to each child's personality.

Grandparents

Involved grandparents can provide a positive influence on your child, especially if you are a single parent. If you recall, earlier in the chapter we mentioned that active grandparents give those children who do not have both a mom and dad at home an academic boost. But the benefits of involved grandparents are not limited to single parents. One of the greatest assets that many grandmothers and grandfathers have to offer is their time. For most parents, the obligations seem endless, and time is a rare commodity. Work, laundry, and meals to prepare—all these responsibilities reduce the opportunities we have to be with our children. And if we are not in the middle of something, our minds often are.

But Grandpa and Grandma usually have fewer demands on their time. In our home, when Grandpa and Grandma walk in, our boys are ecstatic. Grandparents are greeted with open arms, and our children know for the coming hours they will get 100 percent attention. Whether coloring pages, doing puzzles, or simply playing a game of catch, the boys will be fully engaged.

Grandparents can also share their life experiences and give children a different perspective. They can provide an enriching experience by telling their life stories: where they lived, how they worked, or maybe how technology has changed their lives. Nearly every grandparent can tell the story of how they walked uphill to school and home again in waist high snow! Children are eager to peer into the past through the eyes of an adored grandpa or grandma.

Not all children have grandparents to enjoy, but there are often other opportunities available so children can gain the same benefits from interacting with seniors. Most older people adore young children, and time spent with youngsters can brighten their lives. Take a look for suitable persons around your neighborhood or church—maybe even enlist your friend's parents—to give your children a chance to visit with older folks under your supervision. Some senior centers or nursing homes welcome visits from children to talk or play games with the residents. So check for opportunities in your area. It is a win-win situation for children and seniors.

In the end, building solid relationships is a fundamental key to unlocking your child's intellectual potential. Healthy relationships, especially with you, will prepare your child for a bright future.

The Power of Print:

What Reading Can Do
for Your Child

ARLY EXPOSURE TO READING will provide the foundation for later academic success. But there is no need to enroll your preschooler in rigorous academic classes or practice monotonous drills. Your youngster has years to sit at a desk and do homework.

Instead, introduce reading in ways that are best for your preschool child, as we will show in this chapter. The impact can be considerable. In addition to preparing your youngster to start school successfully, you will foster a love for learning that will last a lifetime.

Why Read?

Over the decades, a great deal of attention has been given to learning to read—and for good reason. Without proficient reading skills, a child will not do well in school. Every subject—history, science, math, social studies, and music—is dependent upon reading ability. As a parent, you know this. But what can you do? How can you help your child make the transition from the spoken to the written word?

According to a report prepared by The Center for the Study of Reading for the National Academy of Education's Commission on Public Policy, "The single most important activity for building the knowledge required for eventual success in reading is reading aloud to children. This is especially so during the preschool years."[1] Adriana Bus and Marinus Ijzendoorn from Leiden University in the Netherlands, along with Anthony Pellegrini from the University of Georgia, collected twenty-nine studies that examined the impact of parents reading to their children.[2] Looking at the sum of the research, the team determined that reading to a child regularly results in language growth, emergent literacy, and higher reading achievement.

Next we take a detailed look at the advantages of reading to your preschooler.

Gain One-on-One Time

Reading to your child affords you the opportunity to give your child one hundred percent of your attention, unlike the rest of the day. You put aside the laundry, cleaning, bill-paying—any number of chores that must be finished by the day's end—to be exclusively with your child. And, as most parents can attest, reading to your child is a gratifying experience. When your son or daughter climbs in your lap for a story, there is an emotional closeness between you and your child that strengthens your relationship.

This time together will also give your child a positive reading experience that will shape his or her attitude towards books. We have little doubt as parents that our boys' attraction to books is due to their enjoyable early reading experiences. Our kids spent countless hours in our laps as we paged through all sorts of book, from animal board books to books recounting the tales of Robin Hood. And today, they sleep with their books, right along with their favorite stuffed animals.

But your child's passion for books will transcend the printed pages, for the book is merely a vehicle for learning. Your child's love for books will be transformed into a desire to learn, and the appetite for knowledge is a key to intellectual achievement.

Learn Book Handling

By reading to your child, he or she will learn the basics of book handling and conventions, such as how to hold a book and that you start at the beginning and turn the pages one at a time until the end of the book. Children model the behavior they see, right down to minute details. Reading is no different. At our house, each time Grandma came over, story time would soon follow. And when she went home, our youngest son would pick up a book. Like his grandmother, he, too, would lick his index finger to turn the pages.

Achieve Phonological Awareness

Reading to your little one can help your child achieve phonological awareness—to hear the difference between words, as well as the differences in the syllables and letter sounds. This phonological awareness is a critical skill children must acquire before they learn to read. Children with greater phonological awareness learn to read more quickly, even when IQ is accounted for.[3] Reading rhymes and rhyming stories is particularly helpful for recognizing meter and learning to differentiate word sounds. (We will discuss more about types of reading materials and the advantages later.)

Increase Vocabulary

Reading to your youngster increases his or her vocabulary level. Books contain richer and more varied language than that heard on television or in everyday conversation. For example, there may be words that are regional or from a different time period that you will only find in books: If you live in the city, it's unlikely you will find a "silo" in your backyard; since we live in twenty-first century, chances are you do not have a "moat" around your house.

Donald Hayes and Margaret Ahrens from Cornell University compared words used in children's books to those contained in prime-time television conversations and to the conversation of college graduates.[4] They found that books used 50 percent more rare words. In fact, the researchers concluded that "a child whose language 'diet' is largely restricted to natural conversation and popular television would encounter few instances of the terms which make up the great majority of items used on standardized achievement tests and the most common intelligence tests to assess children's verbal progress and determine academic placement."

Reading a story repeatedly to a child will reinforce the meaning of new words, which helps increase overall vocabulary.[5] And if you stumble on a favorite tale, you will likely hear the request for the same story over and over. A child may even begin to "read" aloud from memory and thus use words from the story that are above his or her current vocabulary level. Eventually these novel words will become part of his or her everyday conversation.

Some research suggests those children who start out early knowing more words increase their vocabulary advantage when they are older. Claudia Robbins and Linnea Erhi from the University of California, Davis, found when children are read stories, those with smaller vocabularies learn fewer words than those with larger vocabularies.[6] This is because those with larger vocabulary have more skills to determine the definition of the word by context. Also, children who already have a greater vocabulary will likely have more factual knowledge to determine the meaning of a word. Unfortunately, this is not good news for children who start out behind in school. Since vocabulary size is associated with academic success, this compounds the problem for children who are struggling as they move up the grade levels; they will likely fall further behind.[7]

Improve Reading Comprehension

Closely related to early vocabulary skills is reading comprehension. Catherine Snow, a Harvard faculty member with over three decades of literacy study, and her fellow researchers determined: "Perhaps the most robust finding in the field of literacy is the high correlation between vocabulary and reading comprehension."[8] Vocabulary has not only been correlated with pre-reading skills such as phonological awareness, but to reading comprehension.[9] Children who have greater vocabularies not only learn to read more easily, but make better readers. By about fourth grade, those with the larger vocabularies have better reading comprehension, and the advantage continues into high school.[10]

Gain Exposure to More Complex and Varied Sentences

While books contain more complex and varied sentence structure than the spoken language, books differ greatly in the details and descriptions they use. For instance, the dialogue between two mad scientists will be different than how a girl would speak to her puppy. The way an author describes a bandit scene in a medieval forest would not be the same as recounting how two boys solve a mystery. In addition to the varied storylines, books are written by authors with their own unique voices and writing styles.

Also, there are stylistic differences between nonfiction and fiction books. Nonfiction books are written with a more direct voice and are not likely to include any dialogue. In fiction works, the writing can be as simple as a short poem or as imaginative and fanciful as *Alice in Wonderland*.

Boost General Knowledge

An increase in overall knowledge is another benefit of reading. The subjects to read about are endless, and the more variety your child is exposed to, the more your child will retain. Since overall knowledge is a component of intelligence, it is safe to say that if you read a wide range of books to your child, you will have a smarter preschooler.

Just as reading a book together enhances both one-on-one time and vocabulary growth, a child's overall knowledge increases as a result of the time spent being with an attentive parent. Not only is it the right time and place to answer your youngster's questions, but you can also interject your own knowledge and experience during story time. Don't hesitate to make the storybook a backdrop for expanded discussion. We will provide specific examples later in the chapter.

Enhance Problem-Solving Skills

Problem-solving skills are cultivated as you read to your preschooler. Many stories present a problem followed by a solution. In a story for a younger child, these problems and solutions are simple: A dog becomes ill and Mom or Dad takes it to the vet; or a car gets dirty and it must be washed.

Children can also see how different abilities and skill sets may get the protagonist into trouble but then may also be used to solve a problem. This is a consistent theme in the *Curious George* series, where agility and curiosity consistently cause the monkey problems, but in the end our furry friend saves the day. For example, in *Curious George Plays Baseball*, George gets into trouble during a baseball game by hitting the balls onto the field.[11] However, at the conclusion of the story he happens to be perched on a flagpole and saves the day by catching a fly ball about to hit a woman in the stands.

For an older child, the problems and solutions in the stories become more complex. For example, in the fairy tale "The Three Little Pigs," our curly-tailed friends illustrate how using different material to construct houses affects how their homes will withstand the wolf's huffing and puffing. First the straw house fails, then the house made out of sticks collapses, but the wolf is unable to blow down the house constructed with bricks. Children can apply principles that they learn from a storyline. In this case, if they are constructing a fort outside, the materials they use will make a difference in how strong it is.

Grow Curiosity

Finally, reading anything to your child shapes personality by fostering creativity and curiosity. Because our sons have been exposed to a variety of reading material early, there is no subject (except geography) that they do not find fascinating. Trips to the library elicit almost as much excitement as trips to the toy store—but fortunately are easier on the pocketbook. As we push our folding shopping cart through the book stacks, two eager boys fill it to the brim in record time. And before the car leaves the parking lot, both boys tear into the books, ready for a new adventure. Your child, too, can discover the magic of books and develop a life-long interest in learning.

Reading to Your Child

Some research suggests that how you read to your child may be more important than the amount of time spent reading.[12] The number of hours parents spent reading to their first-grade children was compared between two groups: those who were considered at-risk readers and those who were accelerated readers. The amount of reading time was nearly the same. But what was strikingly different was how the parents interacted with their children during story time. The parents of the gifted children were far more interactive, both physically and verbally, than the parents of the struggling children.

A seminal reading study by Grover Whitehurst and his colleagues at State University of New York at Stony Brook showed that the manner and style in which you read to children contributes to their language ability.[13] The researchers observed children between the ages of one and three who were read to by their parents over a one-month period. The control group did not change reading styles, whereas the parents of the experimental group were taught specific reading skills. In particular, the parents received the following instructions:

- To encourage the child to speak more often using wh-questions (who, what, where, when, why), as well as open-ended questions.
- To rephrase a child's speech in more detailed terms.
- To provide praise and, when necessary, gently correct a child's mistakes.

Not only did the children in the experimental group demonstrate significant language gains after only one month of reading, but nine months later, they remained ahead.

So when you read to your youngster, make story time interactive. Ask questions, give word definitions, make observations, and clarify the story line. Here are samples of questions to pose during or after the story:

Do you know what this word means?
What do you think will happen next?
Where is _____ going?
What do you think he will do?
What would you do in this situation?
Who is your favorite/least favorite character?
What do you like/dislike about the story?
What happened in the story?
What happened first? Next? Last?
What could be some different endings to the story?

Remember the phrase "a picture is worth a thousand words." Add a few words of your own when you turn to an illustration. Not only can pictures help your child learn colors and shapes, but they can increase your youngster's vocabulary, attention to detail, and critical thinking skills. The next time you turn the page and spy a interesting image or character, pose questions like these to your child:

What color is this?
What letter is this?
Where do you think he is going?
Why do you think she is happy?
Uh-oh. Do you think she knows the fox is hiding behind the tree?
Why are they wearing boots?

The key here is to improvise. Any of the above questions or comments can be expanded, depending upon the content. In particular, be sure to add your own knowledge and experience. For example, if you have just read the latest in the adventures of *The Berenstain Bear Scouts and the Missing Merit Badges*, you might add your own personal experience as a Boy or Girl Scout.[14] Just make sure the questions and explanations are appropriate for the developmental level of your child. If your child has his or her own questions, take the time to fully answer them. If you do not have all the answers, be sure to find them and return later to share what you learned.

We recommend reading to your youngster a minimum of thirty minutes a day. You may wish to break your reading sessions into three periods: ten minutes in the morning, ten minutes after lunch, and ten minutes before bed. This is especially helpful to parents of younger children who may have shorter attention spans. As your child matures, you can increase reading times.

Researchers have verified the importance of daily exposure to books. Claudia Robbins and Linnea Ehri from the University of California at Davis showed that the frequency of hearing stories was correlated with vocabulary size by age ten.[15] And in an article titled "Preschool Literacy Experience and Later Reading Achievement," Hollis S. Scarborough, Wand Dobrich, and Maria Hager published their findings about preschool children through second grade and found that the preschool children who had less experience with books— those who were read to only two to three times per week— became poorer readers in elementary school than those who had a daily experience with books as preschoolers.[16]

Don't limit your reading to books. Read everything. The cereal box, toy instructions, or cookie recipes are all fair game. You will know your child is on the path to reading when he or she begins to ask, "What does this say?"

Generating Reading Interest

Every child has unique interests, and it is not hard to discover what captivates your child. Some children enjoy reading dinosaur or sports books, while others prefer a fairy tale or stories about beloved characters such as Thomas the Tank Engine or Curious George. It is helpful to use subjects your child loves to develop an interest in reading. If reading is fun, your child will want more time to listen to stories. And more hours spent listening to stories means more knowledge, more vocabulary, and a greater chance he or she will become an avid reader.

While you support your preschooler's interest, also guide your youngster to unfamiliar topics or characters. Use familiar material to navigate into unfamiliar territory. Favorite stories can provide a transition from more entertaining fiction works to less-animated nonfiction. For example, "Old McDonald Had a Farm" may be used to encourage reading nonfiction books about farm animals. And if your child likes sports, you might read a biography of a famous athlete; if your youngster enjoys art, check out a book on renowned paintings.

To expose your youngster to more books, you may buy new or used books, trade with other families, or, our favorite, check them out from the library. Weekly trips to the library should be a regular family event. As we just mentioned, it is a good idea to get a mix of old favorites and new discoveries. For example, let your child pick three books, and you add three new selections. You can pique your kid's interest in a new subject by associating it with something already familiar:

This book is about lions, just like we saw at the zoo last week.

We just read a book about airplanes; how about a book on another type of transportation, like boats?

Good reading habits start at home, with the parents. Like most behaviors, children mimic what they see. If you read, your child will want to read. On the other hand, if you are watching endless hours of television, your child will want to do the same. You can even set time aside for individual reading together. Your youngster can turn the pages of his or her book, while you catch up on a novel.

Make reading accessible by having books, magazines, newspapers, and catalogs available on tables, baskets, or open shelves. By allowing your child to peruse reading material daily, you improve his or her chances to be a better reader. If your preschooler is surrounded with books, he or she is more likely to spend more hours reading later in life and consequently have a higher reading ability.

Types of Books

There are many types of books for your youngster to explore, and each has unique benefits. Here are some highlights.

Picture Books

Most children begin their path to literacy with picture books. When using books with pictures, your youngster can develop vocabulary skills by pairing a word with an object. For example, a picture of a cat is next to the word "cat." Beyond learning the word for an object, your preschooler also learns that the printed letters together have a meaning—that the symbols "C-A-T" represent a cat. This is a first step toward learning to read. Later, a youngster will learn the sounds the letters make and will eventually be able to read the word "cat."

The Richard Scarry series are excellent picture books. With each turn of the page, the author explores a new topic. For example on a page with the theme "At the Airport," your child will learn the words "blimp," "jet airplane," and "propeller."[17]

Pictures can also nurture your youngster's creative side. As you turn the pages, have your child use the pictures as cues to make up a story. You will be amused by the imaginative tales that spring from your child. Picture cards, which have letters or words with an accompanying illustration, can also be used to inspire a narrative. Turn each card over one by one as your child creates a story to match the image.

Books that Rhyme

Children's ability to identify the sound letters make is a necessary skill acquisition before reading.[18] Research shows listening to rhyming poems and stories helps children identify letter and word sounds. Donald Hayes, from the University of Maine, tested children ages three through five to determine if reading rhymes would help them identify different word and letter sounds.[19] Two versions of the same story were read to preschoolers; one version rhymed, and one did not. By the conclusion of the study, those who were read the rhyming version could more easily recognize the similarities and differences in the sounds of words. Interestingly, when children listened to stories that rhymed, they were less attentive to the storyline. Instead of focusing on the content, the children listened to the rhyming patterns. As a result, these children had greater understanding of letter sounds, though they were less likely to give the details of the story.

Peter Bryant and his collogues at the University of Oxford also studied the relationship between rhyming skills and later reading ability. They followed four-year-olds for two years and found a strong correlation between children who could detect rhyming words and reading skills. The researchers believe that working with rhymes is helpful when a child is learning to read.[20]

Listening to stories that contain rhyming or made-up words can help children read because it makes the stories more easy to memorize.[21] If you watch a child who has not yet mastered reading "read" a story, he or she will turn the pages and recall the plot by using the pictures as cues. After they commit the story to memory, they start to match the spoken words with the words written on the page. With stories that contain rhyming or made-up words, the words are easier to remember. This gives a child a head start on learning to read. Take, for instance, Dr. Seuss' book *There Is a Wocket In My Pocket*. In this story, the protagonist tells the tale of fictional characters living in his house:

> *Did you ever have the feeling there's a Wasket in your basket?*
> *...Or a Nureau in your bureau?*
> *...Or a Woset in your closet?*[22]

Lastly, metered stanzas and rhyming structure help children identify rhythms. Our youngest son gave us an unsolicited demonstration when he was two. One afternoon while we read "The House That Jack Built," we noticed him tapping his foot to the beat of the Mother Goose rhyme. It was a bit humorous; he appeared unaware the rhyme had struck a rhythmic cord.

Storybooks

Storybooks feature a plot and characters that exercise your child's imagination. They introduce your youngster to a world of make-believe, foreign lands, exotic people, and talking animals. Increased vocabulary size is among the many benefits of storybooks, which is correlated with learning to read as well as reading comprehension, as we discussed earlier.[23]

In order to best develop your child's vocabulary and comprehension, make sure you select books that will challenge your youngster. To reach this goal, it is a good idea to include classic books or tales in the mix. Fairy tales in particular are great. They use words and writing styles not found today that are beneficial in building vocabulary and grammar. For example, here is a colorful description of the difficult early life of Cinderella, which is often lacking in contemporary children's stories:

> *Besides that, the sisters did their utmost to torment her—mocking her, and strewing peas and lentils among the ashes, and setting her to pick them up. In the evening, when she was quite tired out with her hard day's work, she had no bed to lie on, but was obligated to rest on the hearth among the cinders. And because she always looked dusty and dirty, as if she had slept in the cinders, they named her Cinderella.*[24]

Books that have individual chapters, or chapter books, should be added to your child's reading selection. Chapter books are longer; therefore, the characters, scenes, and dialogue are more developed and richly described. We are not recommending that every three-year-old have a steady diet of classic or chapter books. But many five- and six-year-olds do miss out on the rich qualities of these types of literature. You must determine when your child is ready, and then you may want to start reading a page or two, gradually increasing to an entire chapter. If your youngster is not yet ready to sit with you while you read from longer books, try having him or her play with some building toys or draw while you read aloud.

Nonfiction

While fiction takes you on an imaginary adventure, nonfiction expands your child's overall knowledge. Through nonfiction books, your preschooler may find the answers to such questions as:

> *Who were the Pilgrims?*
> *What are submarines?*
> *Where is Ireland?*
> *Why does it rain?*
> *When do bats sleep?*
> *How do apples grow?*

Children's nonfiction differs from adult nonfiction in a couple of significant ways. First, the sentence structure and vocabulary are understandable by the fledgling reader, and the content is less specific and more easily digestible. A five-year-old need not wade through Gibbon's six heady volumes to get a remedial understanding of the Roman Empire. Another distinction is that children's books commonly contain pictures. Pictures help maintain a preschooler's attention, as well as generate interest. Pictures also provide a visual aid to learning. For example, through reading out loud, a child may hear that one difference between a butterfly and a moth is that the butterfly has brighter colors. A picture then visually reinforces the difference, and the youngster is more likely to retain the knowledge.

Newspapers and Magazines

When catching up on your daily news, use the newspaper as a tool to teach current events, geography, weather, and sports. Pick an appropriate article and read it out loud. You may use the article as a catalyst for discussion. For example, you might say, "It looks like there will be a new freeway near us. Do you think that is a good idea?"

Whereas newspapers focus on current events, magazine topics run the gamut from wildlife to architecture. You do not necessarily need to read an entire article, but you may summarize it using pictures as a guide. It is especially exciting for your child to receive his or her own magazines with stories, crafts, puzzles, games, and recipes designed for the younger audience. Here are some good suggestions:

- *Zootles* (ages 2–6). Offers animal pictures, facts, stories, games, and puzzles. Also provides a featured letter, phonic sound, number, or color. For more information, go to www.zoobooks.com
- *Your Big Backyard* (ages 2–7). Created by the National Wildlife Federation with a focus on animals and nature. Includes stories, games, recipes, and crafts. For more information, go to www.nwf.org
- *Highlights High Five* (ages 3–6). Geared towards the preschooler, with read-along stories, poems, finger plays, rhymes, and simple nonfiction. Other features include hidden pictures, cooking, and crafts. For more information, go to www.highlights.com
- *National Geographic Little Kids Magazine* (ages 3–6): Focuses on nature; includes interesting stories, photography, and games. For more information, go to www. nationalgeographic.com
- *Turtle Magazine* (preschoolers) and *Humpty Dumpty* (ages 4–6). Both magazines feature entertaining stories, poems, games, and activities. For more information, go to www.cbhi.org

Audio Books

While not a substitute for reading to your child, audio books can be a blessing when you are busy or your preschooler needs some time alone. You can play a CD or cassette tape of a classic story relatively guilt-free, knowing your child is exercising his or her mind while listening. Instead of watching images on the television, your preschooler must visualize the characters and scenes.

In a study from the University of California, Los Angeles, researchers, using both audiotape and a video production, presented young children with incomplete stories.[25] After the story was stopped, the youngsters were asked to complete the tale. The imaginative responses were compared between those who listened to the audio version versus the children who watched the video version. Those who listened to the audio versions devised more creative conclusions and incorporated more imaginary events, words, and novel characters than those who had watched the video version of the story.

Fortunately there is a plethora of audio material on tapes or CDs, ranging from short stories on tape with an accompanying book to longer chapter books. The narration can be animated and may even include different voices or sound effects. Some stories may be read by a single person without sound effects. With the shorter stories, the child follows the book along with the audio and turns the pages at the sound of a tone. On the other hand, longer stories often do not come with a book and require greater attention abilities from your son or daughter as he or she follows along by listening.

You can purchase audio tapes and CDs, or check them out from your local library. We collected nearly one hundred classic audio stories for our personal library; the kids love to hear these over, and over, and over. We have checked out other audio selections on our weekly visits to the library. Generally we leave with at least two audio tapes per kid. Our younger son prefers the tape and accompanying book, while our older son has graduated to series stories such as *The Box Car Children* and *The Magic Tree House*, as well as chapter books like *Willie Wonka and the Chocolate Factory* and *The Wizard of Oz*.

Math Books

Books that use problem-solving or math concepts such as counting, addition, subtraction, and telling time can make learning fun by including these concepts as part of the story line. Researchers at Boston College found children's math abilities improve when these types of math stories are read, because it makes the math more meaningful.[26] In fact, when youngsters received geometry lessons, those who were taught within the context of a story made greater improvements in their mathematics skills than those who were taught without the help of the story.

Two authors who write these types of stories are Stuart Murphy and Grace Maccarone. In Murphy's *The Best Bug Parade*, he discusses the relative size of a variety of bugs.[27] On the other hand, Maccarone teaches different shapes in her parody, *The Silly Story of Goldie Locks and the Three Squares*.[28]

Time spent reading math stories, or any of the other categories of books, is time well spent. It will set your youngster on the right intellectual path for the rest of his or her life.

Let's Talk:

How Language Skills Contribute to Your Child's Intellect

A TRIP TO YOUR LOCAL GROCERY STORY will reveal how different parents interact with their children. Down one aisle you may find a mother pushing a cart with her preschooler strapped in and hear little verbal communication. Instead, mom is on a mission, focused on gathering the family necessities rather than interacting with her child. Down another aisle you may see a mother fully engaging her child. She may point out the tangerines and the different sizes of soda pop bottles on the shelf, or ask her child what they should get for dinner. *But does it matter?* Will the two mothers' different levels of attentiveness and verbal interaction have a long-term impact on their children's intellect? Absolutely!

Why Talk to Your Child?

Preschoolers learn at an astonishing rate—especially linguistic skills. Although estimates vary, two-year-old children can speak about 200 words, and by age six they know close to 14,000 words.[1] Preschoolers learn not only words at this time, but language syntax rules as well. They learn how to form plurals, change verb forms, and create more complex sentences.[2] Children's expressions evolve from two- to three-word utterances as a toddler, to compound sentences during the preschool years.[3]

Your youngster develops linguistic skills from what he or she hears in the environment—every minute of every day. And you are the teacher, instructing by informal example rather than formal lessons. Whether your child struggles with his or her linguistic ability or is gifted is, in part, up to you. A home rich in language, both in the complexity of sentence structures and advanced vocabulary, will make a significant difference in your child's linguistic development.

When your child hears spoken language, verbal skills as well as comprehension improve. In other words, the more a child hears language, the better he or she can speak and understand what is being said.

Barbara Tizard and her colleagues at the University of London examined the time orphanage children spent interacting with adults; they found those children who had more one-on-one conversations with an adult had greater verbal comprehension.[4] In fact, the youngsters who spent the most time talking with an adult had comprehension levels similar to those children who lived in private homes with their families.

And those kids who have a more extensive vocabulary are better readers, which we also discussed in Chapter 4. Andrew Biemiller from the University of Toronto found that knowledge of oral and written vocabularies accounted for nearly all the variance in reading comprehension in elementary grades one through six.[5] Simply stated, those children who had a greater vocabulary had higher reading comprehension all through grade school.

Elaine Reese from The University of Otago in New Zealand also found a correlation between conversation and literacy skills. She found that children who frequently discussed events that happened on the average of four months prior had even higher literacy skills than children who were read to regularly.[6] These youngsters also had greater vocabulary, story comprehension, and print awareness, which includes such concepts as the printed word has meaning, you read from left to right, and words are constructed with letters.

Experts believe that conversations about past events are important because they allow a child to practice removing him or herself from a present situation, a skill required when reading. In order to read, a child must interpret the text without props or help from his or her immediate environment—reading is an abstract exercise.

Talking about past events can also build memory skills. It is not unsurprising that if you talk with your youngster about things that happened in the past, his or her memory skills will improve—and research supports this.[7]

The National Institute of Child Health and Development (NICHD) also verified the importance of verbal skills by following children from ages three through third grade.[8] They found children who had greater oral skills when they were three years old were able to both sound out and recognize more words by first grade. And by third grade, these children had better reading comprehension.

When to Talk With Your Child

Throughout the day, use every opportunity to speak to your child: when you're driving, on a walk, or in the grocery store. Anywhere, anytime, is right for talking and building your youngster's language skills and vocabulary. Ask questions, make statements, and provide observations. For instance, use the time when making lunch to talk to your child, rather than silently preparing the food:

> *I am hungry. How about you? I am going to make a sandwich. First, I will get two pieces of bread and set them side by side on the plate. Next, I will get a knife and spread the peanut butter and then the jelly on one piece. Then, I put the second piece of bread on top. I have made a peanut butter and jelly sandwich.*

We provide many more practical examples in Chapters 9 and 10.

How to Talk to Your Child

When speaking to your child, do not be reluctant to use words beyond his or her current vocabulary level. In fact, challenging your child's word skills is probably the best way to increase his or her vocabulary. Harvard faculty member Catherine Snow and her colleagues found the greatest predictor of a child's vocabulary level and emergent literary skills is exposure to rare words.[9] And their findings have been corroborated. Two other researchers, Susan Landry, from the University of Texas Health Science Center in Houston, and Karen Smith, from the University of Texas Medical Branch in Galveston, studied the influence of parenting on literacy skills. They concluded, "Of all the parent measures assessed in this study, one of the most important in understanding differences in children's later cognitive competence was the use of rich and varied vocabulary." [10] What was striking in this study was the language variance between homes. In some homes, children heard fewer than one hundred different words per hour from their parents, while others heard more than 500 different words per hour. Likewise, some parents spoke a total of about 200 words per hour, while the most loquacious parents used over 5,000 per hour. The home environments varied wildly, and, as anticipated, so too did the verbal skills the children brought to the start of school. Those with few and less varied words spoken at home were at a substantial disadvantage.

It is easy for preschoolers to learn new words. They are quite adept at deriving the meaning of a word by the context. And the more words they know, the easier it is to derive the definition from the context. At the same time, if you help out with the definition after using a more advanced word, they will more likely retain it. So provide a word's meaning if you suspect that your child does not know it. Make sure your child feels comfortable asking about an unknown word. With the right environment, you will find your curious preschooler is eager to learn.

Since your child learns to talk by modeling what is heard, speak properly. Don't dumb down the conversation with simple sentences or baby talk. It may be tempting to call a horse a "horsie," but your child will learn more by using correct words.

And when your youngster makes a mistake, gently correct him or her by repeating the words or phrases correctly. For example, preschoolers often have difficulty pronouncing certain letters or using the correct verb tense.

CHILD: *I want wunch.*
PARENT: *OK, let's have lunch.*
CHILD: *Look at the picture I drawed.*
PARENT: *What a nice picture you drew!*

Descriptive Language

Likewise, use more complex sentence structure by elaborating on the details and filling your sentences with adjectives and adverbs. For those of you for whom grammar class seems a bit distant, add words that modify or enrich the nouns and verbs.

Instead of:
  Look at the cat!
Try this:
*Look at the gray cat with a long tail. It is running across the
  wet grass.*

And here is a sample of adjectives you could use to describe your kid's cookie.

You have a big cookie!
You have a large cookie!
You have a huge cookie!
You have an enormous cookie!
You have a giant cookie!
You have a humongous cookie!

Here are some adverbs that you can use to describe a child on the playground.

The girl is running fast.
The girl is running quickly.
The girl is running swiftly.

Use a variety of verbs too. For example, here are some verbs used to describe an active bird.

The bird is hopping on the fence.
The bird is jumping on the fence.
The bird is bouncing on the fence.

When your youngster makes simple statements, ask for more details. This helps develop your child's ability to express himself or herself orally and trains his or her mind to look for details.

CHILD: *I met a new friend at the park.*
PARENT: *Oh, I saw her. What was her name? Was she older*
          or younger than you? What did you like about her?
          What did you play together?

Asking Questions About Past Events

As we discussed earlier, talking about past events is correlated with later literacy skills. Here are some ideas:

- Ask open ended questions:
  Who was in your music class today?
  What did you do at Grandma's house?
  Where did we go yesterday?
  When did we last play this game?
  Why was the boy crying?
- Encourage memory:
  How did you make the sand castle?
- Elaborate by introducing new information about the event:
  I saw you playing on the swings, but didn't you also go
  down the slide?
- Add knowledge to the discussion, such as defining words or terms:
  I liked the tractor we saw yesterday. Did you know that
  when I was a little boy, my Grandpa had one on his farm?
  He used it to...

- Relate the event to your youngster or others:
  The little girl you met had a princess t-shirt just like yours.
- Add to your child's fantasy:
  The fish you caught the other day was much bigger than anyone else's.

Math Language

Give math more prominence by using math concepts and terminology with your child. Preschool children who lack experience with math before they start school may be at a disadvantage compared to those who spend more time with mathematics.[11] This is because familiarity makes the concepts concrete. Your son or daughter can learn not only definitions, but applications as well. By incorporating math into your daily routines, your youngster will have a jump-start on peers when ready for formal schooling.[12] Here are some ideas:

- Counting:
  Let's put three teddy bears on the bed. One, two, three.
- Shapes:
  Let's move this train track over here to make an oval.
- Size:
  The orange is bigger than the apple.
- Measurement:
  Which one of these sticks is longer? Shorter?
- Volume:
  Here are two buckets. Which one do you think will hold more sand?
- Weight:
  Which basket is heavier? Lighter?
- Ordinal:
  You can have a drink first, your sister will be second, and I will go third.

- Distance:
  There are two playgrounds. Which one do you want to use?
  The closer one or the farther one?
- Fractions:
  I am breaking this cookie in half.
  I will cut this pizza into four equal pieces. Each piece is
  one-quarter of the pizza.
- Money:
  This is a penny, nickel, dollar...
  I have five pennies. They equal five cents, or one nickel.
- Opposites:
  The dog was wet, but now he is dry.

Time Talk

While a preschooler's ability to understand and tell time is limited, the young mind can grasp the basic concepts of time. As your child gets older, the relationship between units of time will become clearer: A week is longer than a day, or an hour is longer than a second. But do not expect children of this age to fully comprehend time measurements. For example, the preschooler will not understand that there are seven days in a week, or sixty seconds in a minute.

The best way to introduce your preschooler to the concept of time is through everyday conversation, with the help of a clock and a calendar. Here are some suggestions to help him or her understand simple time concepts:

- Seasons
  In the fall, we will go trick-or-treating.
  I am so excited about winter because we will celebrate
  Christmas.
- Calendar units
  In two weeks it will be your birthday. Let's count the days
  on the calendar. It is in November on a Tuesday.

- Days
  Tell Grandma what we did yesterday.
  We are going to the park today.
  Tomorrow, we will go to the birthday party.
- Periods of the day
  What a beautiful morning!
  You can play outside this afternoon.
  Save your picture so you can show your dad when he gets home this evening.
- Time
  We are going to eat lunch at noon. That is when both the big and little hands are on the 12.
  You have ten minutes left to finish eating.

Talking With Others

It is amazing how parents are able to understand their very young children. What is an inaudible garble to the untrained ear, parents not only understand but can also respond to. Other adults may not understand the child's unique pronunciations or individual vocal inflections. By having opportunities to speak with other adults, your child will learn to speak with greater clarity.

Opportunities for adult conversation are plentiful. Your children can speak with relatives, other children's parents, store or library employees, or a waiter at your favorite restaurant. If your children have a question for a staff member, whether looking for the bubble bath at the grocery store or making a request to exchange a toy in their kid's meal for a different one, encourage the conversation. We allow our children to approach a staff member to ask an appropriate question while we wait a few steps back. And when we are with our friends, we make sure the kids ask the other parents when they need something and to say thank you upon leaving.

Foreign Language

It is no surprise that the part of the brain that processes language is strengthened when a person learns a second language. Researchers from the Wellcome Department of Imaging Neuroscience in London, England, found that the left part of the brain is denser in those who are bilingual.[13]

What is surprising is that the brain's increased ability is not limited to language skills. Decades of research consistently show that bilingual children gain in verbal and nonverbal cognitive abilities as well.[14] Penelope Armstrong and Jerry Rodgers from Pittsburg State University studied third-grade students who received half-hour Spanish lessons three times a week for one semester.[15] The children in the experimental groups who had Spanish instruction gained more in language and mathematics than did those children in the control group, who did not have the lessons. What is more, the children in the experimental class who subsequently received one and a half hours *less* of math instruction a week due to the time spent learning Spanish made greater improvements in math than those without the Spanish lessons.

For quite some time, neurologists have known that earlier language acquisition leads to greater fluency. If a child acquires a second language in the preschool years, or before the ages between five to seven, their skills match those of a native speaker.[16] For every year after age seven, the ability to learn a second language and sound like a native speaker decreases, until the age of fifteen. After this point, it is highly unlikely that a person learning a second language will replicate the sounds like a native speaker. The irony is that most schools start offering foreign language classes in high school, when it is too late for the adolescent to attain native fluency. (Of course you can learn the language at this later age, but the native tongue continues to influence the second language.)

And while some studies do show that bilingual children initially lag in verbal skills, they soon catch up to their peers.[17]

Many believe total immersion is required to reach fluency in a second language. Educators define "total immersion" programs as those that teach all subjects in the second language. For a preschool-age child to learn a language, he or she would need to speak regularly with a native speaker. If you are fluent in a second language, or have a grandparent, aunt, uncle, or trusted neighbor readily available, you have the resources for total immersion. In some cities you may find immersion classes for young children. Look through your local phone book or check the Internet for possibilities. Immersion may be unrealistic for most families; but your preschooler need not have full immersion in order to reap the cognitive benefits.

Starting classes early will also provide a diverse cultural experience and set the foundation for foreign language education in the future. You may find some classes offered at your city park and recreation departments, as well as other community groups. Also, there is a plethora of second-language audiotapes, DVDs, and software available for purchase and from the library. But research suggests that while your child may learn some vocabulary, more complex elements of a language, such as proper pronunciation and grammar, will remain elusive.[18]

Talking with your child, in whatever language, remains one of the easiest, yet most effective, things to do to develop his or her intellect. So, do it often, and do it with enthusiasm and a sense of discovery. .

Playtime:

The Benefits of Play

PLATO CONSIDERED children's free play frivolous—and this view remained unchallenged for centuries.[1] However, during the late 1800s, another philosopher named Friedrich von Schiller reexamined whether there was another meaning or purpose to children's play. He theorized that it occurred as a result of surplus energy.[2] Since then, philosophers and psychologists have continued to consider children's play and today agree that the role of play in children's lives is important: "Play no longer appears trivial but is seen as critical for children's development and learning."[3] While there are different theories on play, Piaget proposed children used play to further their cognitive development and understanding of the world around them. He and his colleagues determined four types of play are exhibited during the preschool years.

Types of Play

Practice or Physical Play

Piaget identified the first type of play in which a child engages as practice play, which he named after its repetitive nature.[4] For the infant, practice play is a means to understand his or her world through exploration and experimentation. Researchers believe early play "is an essential precursor of later reasoning and that by engaging in sensorimotor play (or practice play), the infant is laying the foundations of thinking and reasoning."[5] For example, an infant may perform his or her own physics experiment by swatting a hanging toy. As a child's mental abilities and motor skills evolve, so, too, does the complexity of practice play. The preschooler's practice play takes the form of physical activities such as running, climbing, play-fighting, and chasing. At that age, physical play is more helpful in developing fine and gross motor skills than for making cognitive gains. We discuss the benefits of physical play or exercise at length in Chapter 11.

Pretend or Symbolic Play

The most studied type of play is pretend, or symbolic, play, which may be conducted either in a solitary or a social environment. Experts believe pretend play activity may be one of the most important activities during the preschool years and that it should be encouraged.[6] Because he or she is practicing the use of symbols when entering the world of make-believe, this type of play is a powerful tool to develop a youngster's mind. For example, a paper towel roll may be turned into a telescope, or a stick transformed into a sword. The use of symbols is essential for higher level thinking: to learn to talk, a child must understand that words symbolize objects or actions, and to learn to read, a child must realize that letters, when put together, symbolize words.[7]

Problem-solving, too, has been shown to improve through pretend play. Shirley Wyver from Macquarie University and Susan Spence from the University of Queensland demonstrated that pretend play is especially helpful in developing divergent problem-solving, which is the ability to solve problems with multiple solutions.[8] This is the same skill that would enable a person to come up with various ideas during a brainstorming session.

Sandra Russ and her colleagues at Case Western Reserve University followed first- and second-grade children for four years and found that those children who engaged in more fantasy play had greater problem-solving skills.[9] Likewise, Eli Saltz and his associates at Wayne State University explored the relationship between play and intelligence in preschool children.[10] The researchers divided the children into four groups: two play groups, a fantasy discussion group, and a control group. The two play groups engaged in pretend play with adult guidance. One group practiced thematic-fantasy play, in which children played roles based upon selected fairy tales. The other group's play was sociodramatic, in which the children reenacted everyday themes such as visits to the grocery store or doctor. The children in the discussion group heard and discussed fairy tales, while the control group primarily engaged in arts and crafts activities.

Saltz and his colleagues found the youngsters who engaged in thematic-fantasy play made gains in IQ over those in sociodramatic play and those in the discussion group. This conclusion concurs with Russ's finding that play further removed from reality provides more cognitive benefits. But interestingly, it is not merely the variance from reality that is advantageous; role playing adds to the experience. This is evident because those kids who read and discussed fairy tales did not show these cognitive gains.

Children's math skills also appear to benefit from the world of make-believe. Thomas Yawkey from Pennsylvania State University divided five-year-old middle-class children into test and control groups after giving all the children an initial IQ screen to ensure they were intellectually equivalent.[11] The youngsters in the test group engaged in social pretend play over the course of the school year, with such themes as feeding the animals at the zoo and buying food at the grocery store. When the kids had their math skills tested again, those children who engaged in pretend play in a social environment had higher math scores than the youngsters in the group who did not play.

Lastly, play has been shown to correlate with verbal skills. We talked about how important conversations about past situations are for your child's language development in Chapter 5; similarly, pretend play also develops this abstract ability.[12] During pretend play, children use their language skills to create a fictional scene. And by doing so, they strengthen their language skills.

Likewise, Anthony Pellegrini from the University of Georgia verified a relationship between play and reading, writing, and language. He observed six-year-olds over a four-week period during playtime and classified the types of play in which the children were engaged. Pellegrini found that those who played using the highest level of symbolism had the greatest achievement in verbal skills.[13] This again relates to our earlier discussion of reading. If you recall, theorists emphasize that reading requires the use of symbols: The letters together make words that in turn represent things. So by playing, a child practices the use of symbolism, which will help him or her when reading.

Construction Play

A third type of play is construction play, in which children use objects to build and create things. Like pretend play, construction play has been shown to develop problem-solving skills. In one study, Peter Smith and Susan Dutton from the University of Sheffield in England had four-year-old children perform a building task with sticks and a marble. One group of children received training to solve the puzzle, while the other group merely played with the materials. Those children who played came up with more creative solutions than those who were trained.[14]

Construction play is also correlated with higher math and spatial abilities. In particular, researchers at Florida State University followed three- and four-year-old children through high school and found those who played with Legos regularly were more accomplished in math, even when IQ was considered.[15] They scored higher on achievement tests in math, took more advanced math classes, and received higher grades in math. The researchers concluded, "We may clearly state that there is a statistical relationship between early Lego performance among preschool and achievement in mathematics, not seen during the elementary school years but later developing at the middle and high school level."

Game Play

According to Piaget, games with rules are the most evolved form of play. While such games are more predominant in elementary school children's play, preschool-age children engage in them too. As a child becomes older, the games he or she plays become more complex and also more competitive. Games can provide a great forum for social play, building verbal skills as well as providing an opportunity to make up rules and engage in pretend play. Outdoor classics include tag, hopscotch, or Duck, Duck, Goose, while indoor games include board games, card games, dominoes, and dice games. The indoor games are especially useful for teaching skills from counting to letter recognition, as well as improving problem-solving and planning ability. Additionally, a preschooler must learn first about the rules and then how to apply them; as the game progresses, the youngster starts to practice such things as staying on task and working towards achieving a goal. Children also love to make to up their own games and rules for even more creative play.

Parents and Play

Parents can play a significant role in increasing a child's play level. Research has shown that when Mom participates, she increases the complexity of symbolic play.[16] Mom may either add more fantasy to the child's current play theme, or she may introduce novel play themes. Both of these methods will challenge the child's current cognitive ability level and aid in his or her cognitive development. However, be sure not to be overbearing when playing with your child; let him or her direct the play.

Pediatricians Danette Glassy and Judith Romano and the Committee on Early Childhood, Adoption and Dependent Care, suggest the most educational toys are those that foster interaction between parent and child.[17] The toy itself is merely a prop and not as important as the time you spend playing and interacting together. So use playtime to share knowledge. When you build a log cabin together, point out the best construction method, or identify the components of the rescue helicopter, or show how to set the table with a tea set. Make connections for your child by showing how a rhino can easily fit in a boat or that the shape of the house is the same shape as a rectangle.

Toy Collections

Having a large selection of toys available throughout the house will foster different kinds of play. Place them so that your child may access them spontaneously during the day. It may be frustrating to have toys everywhere, but you and/or your child can pick them up throughout the day: before lunch, before leaving the house, before dinner, or before bedtime. Also, take care to rotate toys regularly by bringing those in the closet back out for easy play. This way, your youngster may rediscover toys he or she may have otherwise forgotten.

A large toy collection can be expensive, so if you are on a tight budget, look for used toys at garage sales or second-hand stores. Many cities have consignment stores that specialize in children's clothing, furniture, and toys. Consignment stores sell used toys at a discount or allow you to trade in your children's outgrown toys for store credit to get different toys. You may also check www.ebay.com where there is a large assortment of both new and used toys. You can bid against fellow online auction participants, or, often, you can purchase a desired item for a "buy it now" price.

Have you ever noticed how much fun kids have when playing with other children's toys? If so, you can save a few dollars and still provide novel toys by trading with other families. You can find families to rotate toys with temporarily, or, if you find your child has lost interest in a toy, you can make the exchange permanent. Parents with older children can pass down toys (rather than dispose of them) when their children have outgrown them.

It is easy to feel overwhelmed by the number and variety of toys available on the market today. Yet there are some simple toys that foster creativity, which are great to include in your toy collection. (We will recommend some specific toys later in the chapter.) Such back-to-basic toys require your child to use his or her imagination to create scenes, sounds, and voices for the toy, rather than depending upon a pre-programmed chip and a set of batteries for entertainment.[18] Children engage in more creative play when the materials are less realistic.[19]

The cardboard box is a "toy" that has been a staple in American homes for generations. How many times have you seen a preschooler open a new toy, only to have more fun with the box it came in? Well, save the box! If the box is large enough, cut out a door and a window so your child has a new playhouse for a while. Blankets and sticks are also construction favorites. With the help of blankets and either clotheslines or furniture, children have been "building" forts for generations.

The possibilities for creating imaginary scenes without any toys at all are endless. Our favorite came from our youngest son's creative drama class. The teacher had all the children go on safari. She and the kids donned an imaginary hat, boots, and binoculars. Then, with an imaginary rope, everyone climbed an imaginary mountain. The real excitement occurred when the kids spotted all sorts of animals. The youngsters were so thrilled you would have thought a real tiger or elephant was in the room! But you do not need to take a class to incorporate play without toys or props. For example, you can stretch your child's imagination by creating a pretend pot with your arms. Then make a soup by peeling, cutting, and stirring the imaginary meat and vegetables. Try to come up with some of your own ideas for playing without toys or props.

Not only can children use imaginary props, but they often create imaginary companions as well. Some parents might worry if their child fabricates a friend—they may believe their son or daughter will lack the social skills to interact with their peers. But preschool children who have imaginary friends do not differ from those without invisible companions in their ability to relate with peers.[20] However, if your son or daughter packs a suitcase for an invisible companion on the way to college, there may be a cause for concern.

In the end, we are not suggesting that you dispose of all electronic toys; however, we do ask that you make sure your child has a balance of toys that encourage more imaginative play. As parents ourselves, we have discovered it is more difficult to find toys today that are not battery-operated. In fact, just the other day we opened a new Lego set for one of our sons—and even it required batteries!

Now it's time to offer you some of our favorite, classic, and must-have toys for today's kids. We will do so based upon the category of play. Make sure that you have some available in your home from each category of play.

Pretend Play Toys

With her doctor kit, one little girl loves to give her stuffed animals complete physicals. She checks their heart rates and temperatures, then closely examines their ears and eyes. Our son regularly affixes his red bandana around his neck, and then Superman streaks though our house faster than... well, we would prefer. Your son or daughter will likely discover his or her own way to facilitate pretend play.

Many role-playing kits to enhance your child's play are available right off the shelf, including kitchen sets, doctor kits, plastic food, and dolls. But a trip to the toy store may not be required if you have the time and creativity to make your own: Mom's old dress and heels can transform your child into a princess, or a lumberjack can appear with the help of dad's flannel shirt and work gloves. Keep last year's Halloween costumes handy; your preschooler can be a lion or a superhero all year long.

Choose toys that promote role-playing, and take your child to an imaginary place with novel characters. There are many good choices that often come as a set: house, farm, store, and fire station, just to name a few. One way to pique your child's interest in history is to include toys that return the young mind to a prior era, such as castle, pirate ship, and Wild West sets.

Here are some ideas, props, and toys that encourage pretend play.

- Old clothes, hats, purses, jewelry, scarves, and shoes
- Halloween costumes
- Paper pads, notebooks, pencils, and pens for various role playing props such as menus, receipts, prescriptions, and school work
- Play food
- Toy dishes, cookware, and kitchen appliances
- Toy vacuum cleaner, broom, mop, and dustpan
- Cash register and play money
- Toy telephone or non-functioning phone or cell phone
- Dolls, clothing, stroller, furniture, and other accessories
- Doctor, nurse, veterinarian kits
- Cowboy clothes and accessories
- Pretend swords, laser guns, and other toy weapons (based on your family's personal philosophy)
- Chalk and chalkboard
- Toy mowers and garden tools
- Toy tool kits
- Toy barbeque grill and accessories
- Toy camping set

Some examples of sets that typically include both figures/characters and the setting to encourage pretend play follow.

- Construction sets
- Car or truck sets

- Train sets
- Animal and farm/zoo sets
- Dinosaurs
- Circus
- Police, fire, and rescue cars and accessories
- Superhero characters
- Pirates, ship, and accessories
- Knights, castle, and accessories
- Action hero and military figures
- Cowboy and Wild West sets
- Fashion dolls, house, clothes, and furniture
- Robots and space characters
- Little People sets
- Weebles

As we suggest earlier in the chapter, make sure to exchange roles when you play with your child. Take turns as the cashier and customer, doctor and patient, waiter and patron, and other pretend roles. Include props that encourage your youngster to "read" or "write." For example, make a menu from construction paper when playing "restaurant," or have your child use a pad of paper for "writing" out a prescription while playing "doctor."[21]

Construction Play Toys

Take a casual stroll through a toy department, and you will find an endless selection of building toys. Sets of Legos, Lincoln Logs, and blocks can be used to create structures such as cabins, houses, bridges, or towers. Other building toys create a specific design or character. For example, you can make Spiderman with a Mega Blocks Characters set, or with Lego Designer Sets you can build a rescue helicopter.

Most building sets include step-by-step instructions. By following them, your child develops the ability to focus on a task, concentrate, and think sequentially. On the other hand, all building sets allow children to deviate from the directions, limited only by their imagination.

Following is a list of some building toys and sets; pay attention to the age suggestions on the packages.

- Wooden blocks
- Foam blocks
- Corrugated blocks
- Gears building set
- Marble building sets
- Lincoln Logs
- Tinker Toys
- K'nex sets
- Erector sets
- Mega Blocks
- Lego Duplo
- Lego Designer sets

A construction toy almost in a class of its own is the puzzle. Children who are gifted in math are also great at identifying patterns, so what better way to practice with patterns than working a jigsaw puzzle.[22] But how a child solves a puzzle differs by age. Younger preschoolers approach the puzzle less systematically than their older peers. They typically look for pieces that have like colors, rather than sorting by shape. On the other hand, older preschoolers approach solving the puzzle more systematically. They usually begin with identifying and grouping the puzzle pieces by characteristics: the edges first, then the colors. They may make a pile of the green pieces that create a field or blue pieces that form a lake. Next they examine the pieces with more discriminating eyes: pieces of sky containing land make up the horizon. They practice spatial abilities when identifying the shape of the missing puzzle piece, then rotating the pieces to fit. During this time, their young minds are constantly working to complete the image of the puzzle.

Jigsaw puzzles range from simple—the ones with handles on each piece—to those with a thousand pieces or more. Match the puzzle complexity to your youngster's ability. Include a variety of puzzle themes: letters, numbers, animals, geography, occupations, and vehicles are intriguing for a preschooler.

We recommend letters as one puzzle theme every preschooler should have. Letter knowledge is a necessary prereading skill and has been shown to predict later reading abilities.[23] And what better way to learn the alphabet than by solving puzzles? Letter puzzles have two formats: those which have pieces in the shape of letters, and puzzles with letters imprinted upon them. Either variety is great, but our boys have found the puzzles with letters and a picture of an object beginning with the letter especially captivating.

Games

Video games are ubiquitous. Many homes in America have amassed a substantial collection. Unfortunately, hours are often consumed on these games that had previously been reserved for more simple games, such as cards and board games. So rather than play the latest software game, pull out a deck of cards from the bottom of your drawer or dust off one of your board games sitting in the back of the closet.

Board games, card games, dominoes, and dice games teach skills from counting to letter recognition, as well as improve problem-solving and planning abilities. Additionally, your preschooler must first learn the rules and then how to apply them. As the game progresses, your youngster will practice staying on task and achieving a goal. Help him or her with strategy. For example, if your young player makes a poor move, you can point out a better one; or, when it is your turn, share your winning strategy. You will find that your youngster will learn quite quickly and may soon emerge the victor. Teach your child as you go.

> *I rolled a 3.*
> *If I roll a 2, I capture your man.*
> *I owe you $2. Here is $5; you can give me change of $3.*
> *I need to draw the letter "c" and then I can spell "cat."*
> *That was a good move, but a better move would be this one, because...*

Make sure to start with simpler games, and gradually add more complex games as your child matures. There are classic games available, as well as junior versions of old favorites that are aimed at younger players. You can also modify the rules for younger children. For example, our son played Uno when he was five, even though the recommended age is seven. We just removed the reverse cards and didn't keep score. He had a great time matching the colors and numbers. Here are some suggested card and board games for your preschooler that are readily available at most retail stores that sell toys. Specialty stores or online stores may have an even greater selection of unique games.

- Old Maid
- Go Fish
- Crazy Eights
- Uno
- Skip-Bo
- Dominoes
- Checkers
- Chinese checkers

- Bingo
- Don't Spill the Beans
- Ants in the Pants
- Cootie
- Mousetrap
- Hungry Hippos
- Let's Go Fishin'
- Don't Break the Ice
- Chutes and Ladders
- Hi Ho! Cherry-O
- Candy Land
- The Memory Game
- Sequence for Kids
- Operation
- Boggle Jr.
- Scrabble Jr.
- Monopoly Jr.
- Clue Jr.
- Trouble

Playing Outdoors

Outside playtime has diminished as our cities have grown; there are fewer natural areas, more traffic, and a greater fear of predators. Additionally television, DVD, and video games all consume time that in the past was dedicated to outdoor play. But by playing outside, your youngster can incorporate all the different types of play: physical play, construction play, pretend play, and games.

Most obviously, the great outdoors is far better suited for physical play that develops gross motor skills than is rough-housing inside. It is possible to develop these skills while in the house, but it may involve the disturbing sight of your child jumping on the sofa or siblings chasing each other from room to room. Outside there are trees to climb, yards to run through, and balls to catch. Fewer constraints will allow your child to play freely, enhancing creativity.

Both outdoor construction play and physical play can also develop your preschooler's analytical skills. Your child can experiment with volume while filling and emptying buckets in the sandbox or discover that a bigger child will go down the slide faster than a smaller one. Problem-solving skills can by enhanced by building a tunnel, fort, or castle. And your preschooler can learn about science when he or she goes on a nature excursion and collects leaves and pinecones, or observes the ants as they gather food and material for their hill.

Pretend play outdoors occurs naturally for preschool-age children. Your child feels free to engage in role-playing when engaging an imaginary enemy, or when two buddies look out from the highest playground structure in search of pirate ships. As parents, over the years we have seen our children engage in pretend play for hours as they acted out diverse roles and characters.

Outdoor game-playing can feature elements of both pretend play and physical play. Preschool children love to create elaborate rules to enhance their playtime. For instance, when using rocks and sticks as goods for their imaginary store, they may create rules to display and exchange goods. Physical play also can incorporate rules, as when children designate "base" as they play tag or create a rule to "unfreeze" a tagged player.

Try to allow at least thirty minutes a day for outdoor free play, as the weather permits. You can take turns supervising children with trusted neighbors. If you live in a big city where outdoor activities may be more difficult, allow time to go to the park.

Here are some great outdoor activities for the preschooler.

- Climbing playground structures
- Riding a tricycle or bicycle
- Riding scooters
- Bouncing on a pogo stick
- Playing hopscotch
- Playing tag
- Playing Hide and Seek
- Jumping rope
- Playing any game with a ball
- Playing with Hula-Hoops
- Playing jacks
- Making art with sidewalk chalk

We live in sunny Arizona, where the weather can be a scorching 110 degrees or more three months out of the year. You, too, may live in an area where weather can be unsuitable for outdoor play some of the year. Here are some ways that your child can still benefit from active free play, in harmony with or in spite of the weather.

- Swimming
- Playing in the snow
- Bowling
- Roller skating
- Ice skating, snow shoeing, or skiing
- Indoor climbing structures, such as the ones found at some fast food restaurants
- Indoor mall play areas
- Indoor bounce play places

Playgroups

Playgroups provide socialization and age-appropriate play for young children and usually consist of two or more children with parental supervision. The children are typically of similar ages, although the presence of children of various ages can also be beneficial. A playgroup usually meets once a week at a park or a member's house or may meet for a planned activity such as a trip to the zoo or museum. The group provides a youngster with a consistent set of children so he or she is comfortable enough to learn, trust, share, and grow together.

By joining a playgroup, parents can shape a child's peer relationships. Gary Ladd and Beckie Golter from Purdue University verified the importance of a parent's influence on peer relations in their research article titled "Parent's Management of Preschooler's Peer Relations: Is it Related to Children's Social Competence?"[24] They studied how parents can shape their child's behavior by guiding their playmate selection and interactions. Ladd and Golter found that parents who take a more active role in arranging their child's peer relations had youngsters who were better socially adjusted. For boys in particular, those who had parents that were more involved in choosing their child's companions had "greater peer acceptance and lower levels of peer rejection in school."

Pediatricians recommend starting your youngster in a playgroup between the ages of two and a half to three, which is when children move from parallel play, where they play independently in a group setting, to cooperative play, when children play together.[25] During parallel play, children may copy the toys or the styles of play the other children use, but for the most part, they play independently. On the other hand, during cooperative play, there is more interaction between the kids; they learn social skills such as sharing and working together to accomplish a task. They may work together to create imaginary scenes and characters, to dig a tunnel, or to build a toy house. Some enterprising youngsters may create a supermarket at the playground and barter with shells, rocks, and sticks, while others rely on the time-tested game of cops and robbers.

Starting your youngster in a playgroup sooner than two-and-a-half years old will certainly not do any harm, and children may indeed still learn from one another. But starting children much earlier serves more as a support group for the moms than a tool to help a younger child develop social and cognitive skills.

In a playgroup, the benefits of parental supervision are twofold. First, a young child feels more comfortable playing and exploring with mom or dad nearby. A child with a secure attachment will return to mom or dad for "emotional refueling" during playtime, then resume playing either alone or with his or her peers. On the other hand, if a parent is absent, even a child with a secure attachment may be too upset to engage other children or play.

Secondly, an accompanying parent provides an immediate disciplinary figure to resolve disputes and thus shape a child's social behavior. For example, a parent may teach a child to share a toy or to be courteous by thanking another child. As children become older, they need less immediate supervision, because they have developed social skills and are able to work out problems on their own.

Playgroups provide an opportunity for children to challenge one another in a helpful way. For example, your son or daughter is likely to show less trepidation when attempting to climb playground equipment if he or she sees another child successfully navigating the bars and slides, or may copy a more elaborate sand castle that an older child built or learn a more advanced vocabulary word from another youngster. With children of various ages in a playgroup, not only do the younger children learn from the older boys and girls, but the level of play increases for the younger children when they play with older kids.[26] At the same time, the older children benefit from the mixed ages. They build confidence in their abilities and improve social skills by playing with younger playmates. For example, when interacting with younger peers, not only may they show a child how to play "store," but they may learn to be more patient and understanding with younger kids.

To start a playgroup, begin with the people you interact with regularly: friends, neighbors, people at the park, parents in classes, or moms you meet during story time at the library. Churches, homeowner associations, and recreation and community centers within your neighborhood provide an opportunity to create playgroups by advertising with a flyer or ad. Mother's organizations, such as the MOMS Club at www. momsclub.org, have playgroups already established. A quick search online or in your local parenting magazines can also help you find other playgroups in your area.

Time Alone

Finally, provide time for your child to play, read, and think without the influence and direction of media, other children, or adults. Kenneth Ginsburg and the Committee on Communications and the Committee on Psychosocial Aspects of Child and Family Health, recommend "Free play as a healthy, essential part of childhood...all children are afforded ample, unscheduled, independent, non-screen time to be creative, to reflect, and decompress...{While} parents can certainly monitor play for safety, a large portion of play should be child driven rather than adult directed."[27] For your youngster, time alone may be difficult at first. But the short-term discomfort for you and your child will pay big dividends in the future. Time alone will help your child be more independent, self-initiating, self-directing, creative, and better able to concentrate on a task. If you are successful, you may avoid the phrase every parent dreads: "I am sooo bored."

Your child will gain a sense of accomplishment while spending time patiently working on a building set or reading books, while peers struggle to occupy themselves between videos. Try ten minutes of alone time initially, and increase the time to one hour per day as your child grows and matures.

Regardless of whether your youngster plays alone or with parents or peers, play is very important for your child's cognitive development—so make sure you child experiences plenty of free play.

The Electronic Age:

Do TV and Computers Really Help?

TELEVISION IS PREVALENT in society: more than 99 percent of American homes have at least one set, and the programs available seem endless.[1] Many families have long since retired their rabbit ears for satellite service, which can provide more than 280 stations.[2] And when nothing piques your interest among the hundreds of choices available on the television, a movie is often within easy reach. Video or DVD players are found within most homes, along with personal movie collections, to entertain us at the push of a button. When we tire of these, there are plenty available to rent or borrow: movie rental stores, grocery stores, even libraries are stocked with collections.

If you have not checked with your local library, you will be surprised that the number of videos and DVDs in their collection often rivals the fictional book selections. And with all that is available for the television set in the family room, there are still other screen options: for example, PlayStation, GameCube, and/or Xbox for playing the latest video games. Hours can be consumed with these new goodies.

Computers, too, are prevalent in homes. Nearly three out of four households have a personal computer perched on a desk in a home office or a laptop that can be a companion throughout the house or on vacation.[3] Through our computers, we access the Internet to search for any subject we want, read the news, play a game, or communicate with friends. The computer can be used to learn French, design landscapes, or to make a greeting card. There are computers in schools to satisfy the demands of parents and educators who believe it is critical that our youngsters start using a computer early, lest they fall behind.

Here are some national statistics illustrating the prevalent use of electronic media by our youngsters.

- Children before the age of three watch an average of 2.2 hours of television per day.
- Children between three to five years of age view an average of 3.3 hours of television each day.
- Two-thirds of children live in a home where the television is on all or most of the time.
- Thirty-six percent of children have a TV in their bedroom.
- Forty-five percent of parents say that if they have something important to do, they will use the television to occupy the child while they finish the task.
- Forty-eight percent of children under the age of six have used a computer.
- Twenty-seven percent of four- to six-year-olds spend an average of one hour per day on the computer.[4]

But is your child smarter because of all those hours spent behind the TV or computer?

"Educational" Television

There is a variety of educational programming available today. In fact, the Federal Communications Commission, or FCC, has established a Three-Hour Rule that requires stations to air three hours of regularly scheduled programs that are "... 'specifically designed' to serve the educational and informational needs of children."[5] The FCC differentiates "specifically designed" from "primary purpose," saying the program must also be entertaining and attractive to children, but still the educational and informational purpose must be more than "an incidental goal."[6] However, the FCC provides an ambiguous definition of educational and informational programming; i.e., "... programming that furthers the positive development of children sixteen years of age and under in *any* respect, including the child's intellectual/cognitive or social/emotional needs."(Italics ours.)[7]

So when you tune into a program designated as "educational," your child may not be getting the education you intended. Not only may the programming stray from fundamentals such as counting or letter recognition for the sake of entertaining, but anything promoting development of the child, including instruction on social or emotional topics, is fair game.

Sesame Street

To look at the impact of television, we start with the program that has become synonymous with educational TV for youngsters: *Sesame Street*. No other show has run as long, has as many viewers, or has been studied as thoroughly. By 1996, 95 percent of children by age three in 140 countries had viewed the show.[8]

Nearly all American homes had television by the end of the 1960s, and many children tuned in regularly.[9] The time was right for a new type of children's programming. Producers believed they could create a captivating educational program that would reach this audience that included young viewers of all social economic groups. In the spirit of Lyndon B. Johnson's Great Society, *Sesame Street* was intended to level the playing field for those underprivileged children who lacked the resources of their middle-class counterparts. Although *Sesame Street* was not the first child's program to be aired, it was unique because it had goals for the young viewers. First and foremost was to prepare children ages three to five across all socioeconomic backgrounds to be more school-ready.[10] And beyond teaching the basics, such as letter and number recognition, programmers presented a pro-social message that would include cooperation, discrimination, and self-esteem, to name a few.[11] Funded by government monies, as well as corporate and private grants, *Sesame Street* was born. And the rest, as they say, is history.

Advocates of *Sesame Street* point to studies that show correlations between viewing the show and benefits that include increased vocabulary, greater general knowledge, and improved school-readiness as evidence of its effectiveness as a teaching tool.[12] In one of the most comprehensive studies on television viewing, Daniel Anderson and his colleagues at the University of Massachusetts observed 635 preschoolers from Topeka, Kansas, and Springfield, Massachusetts, using a combination of video recorders and diaries.[13] Years later, the adolescents were asked about their academic achievement, reading activity, and levels of math and science classes. Those who had the higher grades, read more, and enrolled in higher level math classes had watched more informational TV, in this case, *Sesame Street*. This study partitioned the children by sex and found that boys who watched *Sesame Street* did better later in school. On the other hand, there was no correlation between the number of hours viewed by girls and their grades or the rigor of math and science classes taken.

The researchers did not speculate about the difference between the boys' and girls' later achievements, but one possible explanation is young boys may spend less time on reading or other activities that groom them for future academic success than their female peers. At this age, it is generally more difficult to keep boys attentive during sit-down activities; boys seem always eager for action. Because boys are often more active, parents may chose to do fewer sit-down learning activities with them such as reading or board games, and as a result, the boys get short-changed. In the aforementioned study, *Sesame Street* may fill this educational void for the boys.

If you have spent any time in the classroom with preschool children, you might notice a difference in activity levels between the boys and the girls—we certainly have. When it was craft time in Sunday school, Renee (the children's teacher) had the children make characters using marshmallows, pretzel sticks, and frosting. For the first few minutes, the children worked diligently, creating the little candy people. But it was not long before the boys began launching marshmallow rockets or simulating wrestle-mania by smashing their half-completed figures together, whereas the girls continued construction until their marshmallow masterpieces were complete.

Another possible explanation why boys may benefit more from educational programming could be that boys tend to be more visual. The pictures along with the audio help boys learn. But rather than sit your little boy in front of Big Bird and the gang, why not provide your own visual enhancements, such as books with colorful illustrations and engaging toys?

In the end, Anderson and his team at the University of Massachusetts concluded television programming in itself is neither good nor bad, but rather it is the content of the program that correlates with later behaviors. They found children who watched educational television did better in academics and were not only more involved in extra-curricular activities, but were more creative and less aggressive.

But as the researchers acknowledged, this study does not prove watching educational television *causes* later behavior. The study is observational—the conclusions are based upon observation alone. The researchers looked at adolescent achievement to see if there was a correlation with early television viewing habits. The fact that more educational television was correlated with higher grades or more reading does not necessarily mean that watching the program caused the higher grades. Instead there may have been other factors that contributed, such as a better home learning environment or parents who may place a higher value on intellectual achievement.

To show a causal relationship, a study must be experimental. An experimental design would include two groups of "equivalent" children—a control and a test group—and researchers would change only one variable. So in this case one would be a group of children that viewed *Sesame Street*—a test group—and the other a control group of kids who refrained from watching the show. After the conclusion of the experiment, the results would determine whether *Sesame Street* changed behavior or improved an intellectual measurement; i.e., IQ, verbal ability, math grades, etc.

Another problem with the study is the failure to take into account individual characteristics of a child, such as intellectual ability or temperament. For example, as discussed earlier, IQ has been shown to be a predictor of academic success, but many researchers do not compensate for this factor in their analyses of television's impact on later behavior.

Some studies do not show a positive correlation between watching *Sesame Street* and academic skills, however. Researchers from the University of Missouri, Columbia, studied data collected from a national survey of 22,782 children that followed from first through third grades.[14] The researchers found watching *Sesame Street* "is negatively correlated with reading and math achievement: those children who spent more time watching the program had lower math and reading scores by third grade."

Unfortunately, nearly all the studies on *Sesame Street* have been observational; there has been little done experimentally to provide a causal link between the program and later behavior. One exception was an experimental study in Mexico City on day care.[15] But no long-term effects of viewing were studied, and the sample little resembled American youngsters, who are more likely to benefit from an enriched home environment, along with a host of other advantages.

Still, if we look at all the available data objectively, it is likely a child could acquire some skills from watching *Sesame Street*, such as learning letters or numbers. But in other respects, educational viewing may not benefit all children. In an article titled "Is the Medium the Message?: An Experimental Comparison of the Effects of Radio and Television on Imagination," Patricia Greenfield and her colleagues at the University of California, Los Angeles, evaluated the impact of viewing educational programming on children's creativity.[16] Greenfield noted the *overall* effect of watching on the children's imagination was positive, but the youngsters who benefited most were less imaginative to start with. In fact, the television program in which children showed the most gains in creativity, *Mr. Rogers*, actually had slightly negative effects on the more imaginative kids.

So as authors and parents, we remain cool to the idea of preschoolers spending many hours behind the TV screen, even when the content is educational. Our primary reason for limiting screen time is that those early years will establish viewing habits for life. Just as you teach good eating habits early, or instill the importance of exercise for maintaining a healthy life style, you also establish television viewing habits. And these habits established during youth are very difficult to change.

Dimitri Christakis, a prolific researcher on the effects of media on children, and colleague Fredrick Zimmerman, both from the Child Health Institute at the University of Washington, observed the viewing patterns of children during the first four years of life.[17] They confirmed that reducing or limiting television viewing for these children by the age of six proved to be a challenge. In fact, they found "reducing or limiting TV viewing in older children may meet resistance, a barrier that may prove difficult or indeed insurmountable for many parents." While the reason for this is not entirely understood, there is evidence that people become dependent on television-watching as a means to alleviating stress.[18] Even children as young as four may use the television to eliminate unpleasant feelings such as sadness. But whether TV viewing is addictive in the strictest sense remain controversial.

Although there was a correlation between types of programming the child viewed as a youngster—for example, those who viewed educational television in the preschool years tended to watch informational programming as adolescents—the strongest correlation was between the hours viewed as a preschooler and the number of hours watched later. Those who watched the most hours as young children also watched more hours later in life.[19]

There are also other non-educational issues about *Sesame Street* you should consider before tuning in. From the start, the objectives of *Sesame Street*'s producers went beyond teaching children the basics such as letter and number recognition. The producers wanted to deliver a pro-social message, and some issues that *Sesame Street* has addressed over the years include death, love, marriage, pregnancy, and divorce.[20] As authors and parents, we believe these topics are best introduced and discussed within the family. We feel parents should be the ones who introduce these topics and explain the relevance to their children's lives, not a television program producer, or even Big Bird.

Finally, if you have young children, you know how impressionable they are. They emulate any and all behavior around them. Now turn on *Sesame Street* and watch the Cookie Monster. Do you see him as an inspiration, equipping your child with the intellect to wrestle with the great philosophical questions of life? Or even in the short-term: do you really want him sitting at your dinner table, with his broken English and poor eating habits to boot? We don't.

General Television Viewing

Whereas the prior research looked specifically at educational programming for the preschool child, the following studies correlated general programming with later outcomes. These results are less than inspiring.

Although researchers have stopped short of attributing viewing hours to attention deficit hyperactivity disorder, or ADHD, television viewing has been shown to be associated with attention problems. Dimitri Christakis and his colleagues at the University of Washington found a statistical relationship between viewing hours and subsequent attention problems: Those children who watched 5.1 hours a day at age one, or 6.5 hours a day at age three, had a 28 percent greater chance of having attention problems by age seven.[21]

Likewise, Eugene Geist from Ohio University and Martie Young from Northwestern Oklahoma State University considered the impact of TV on children's attention levels in their research article titled, "The Effect of Network and Public Television Programs on Four- and Five-Year-Olds' Ability to Attend to Educational Tasks."[22] Geist and Young divided four- and five-year-old children into three groups: One watched *Mister Rogers' Neighborhood*; another watched *The Mighty Morphin Power Rangers*, and the control group watched no television. Instead, the control group children spent time playing with instructional materials such as Play-Doh, finger paints, Legos, and math games. In the television-watching groups, the television was cut off after thirty minutes of viewing, and the children were observed in free play. They then were rated by how long they stayed on a particular task and how many different tasks they performed. The children who watched *Mighty Morphin Power Rangers* were less attentive than either the group of children who watched *Mister Rogers' Neighborhood* or the control group: They switched from task to task more often and spent less total time on each activity. The researchers found no significant difference in attention between the children who watched *Mister Rogers'* and the control group who played.

Geist and Young note that the ability to pay attention can be improved with practice, much as exercise builds muscle strength. In fact, kids' attention will improve most when they are challenged slightly beyond their current ability levels— but television, especially action programming, seldom provides this opportunity. This comes as no surprise, because the goal of the television program writer is to maintain a child's attention during the show, rather than challenge a youngster's current attention level and develop his or her attentive ability. And the television commercial writer's motive is to keep a youngster entertained long enough to sell a product during the commercial.

Research suggests general viewing may lead to long-term attention problems. A team from the Dunedin Multidisciplinary Health and Development Research Unit in Dunedin, New Zealand, found long-term attention problems were related to early childhood viewing.[23] Starting when the children were age three, the researchers assessed the children's ability to pay attention every two years. The team found "that a greater number of hours of childhood viewing was associated with attention problems in child adolescence," even when considering early attention problems, cognitive ability, and socioeconomic status.

As attention problems correlate with long hours of television, so too do negative behavior and poor school performance. Nary Shin from Michigan State University looked at 1,203 children between the ages of six and thirteen and found "the more time children spend watching television, the more impulsively they behave, and eventually they show a decrease in academic achievement."[24] Another survey by The Kaiser Family Foundation underscored the troubling relationship between television viewing and reading: Kids who come from homes that have the television on most or all of the time were less likely to read by age six than those who came from homes with the TV on fewer hours.[25]

Another study by the Dunedin Multidisciplinary Health and Development Research Unit found those who watch more hours of television were less academically accomplished. The team followed more than 1,000 children and recorded their television viewing hours from ages five through age fifteen.[26] When the children were twenty-six years old, the researchers assessed the education level of the individuals. They found watching television was associated with a lower level of education independent of intelligence, family socioeconomics, and childhood behavioral problems. Furthermore, they concluded, "These findings offer little support for the hypothesis that a small amount of television is beneficial, whereas a lot is harmful."

Researchers have also found that those children who come from homes with many viewing hours also experience less enriched home environments. Angela Clarke and Beth Kurtz-Costes from the University of North Carolina observed the viewing habits of preschool-age children, their school readiness, and the quality of their home environments, considering factors such as the number of available children's books and maternal instruction. Those children who were heavy TV viewers had homes with fewer books and moms who were less interactive and less instructive. The youngsters also had poorer academic skills to start school.[27]

Finally, three researchers from the University of Texas considered what impact children's viewing habits had on other activities. The researchers studied the television diaries of 1,712 children through age twelve who had their television viewing recorded throughout the school year by their primary caregiver. The team found that children who watched more television spent less time with other family members, and, more interestingly, they engaged in less creative play. This was especially true for preschool children.[28]

Appropriate Viewing

When considering screen options for your child, the key is quality programming and minimal exposure. In a 2001 Policy Statement in the journal *American Academy of Pediatrics*, pediatricians have developed guidelines for parents that include the following:

- Discourage television viewing for children younger than two years of age, and encourage more interactive activities that will promote proper brain development, such as talking, playing, singing, and reading together
- For children over two years old, limit children's total

media time to no more than one to two hours of quality programming per day
- Monitor the shows children and adolescents are viewing. Most programs should be informational, educational, and nonviolent
- Encourage alternative entertainment for children, including reading, athletics, hobbies, and creative play
- Remove television sets from children's bedrooms.[29]

This last point—keeping televisions out of your child's room—is a good idea for several reasons, the most obvious being supervision. It is more difficult to keep an eye on what your youngster is viewing when he or she is holed up in a bedroom. If the television is in a common living area, you can listen with one ear to ensure that not only does your child stay with the programming you intended, but that programming also meets your expectations. If you recall, what the FCC identifies as "educational programming" may have education as a secondary goal, with the primary focus being entertainment. For this reason, it is a good idea to keep up with the shows your children are viewing. Even if you are not watching with your child, at least be aware of the general format and objectives of the show. Finally, children who have televisions in their bedrooms watch an average of 5.5 more hours a week.[30] We doubt they are glued to re-runs of *Sesame Street*.

Director of Research Douglas Gentile of the National Institute on Media and the Family, along with a team of researchers, surveyed 365 pediatricians to determine what doctors recommended in their practice. They found, "Pediatricians almost universally believe that children's media use negatively affects children in many areas, including aggressive behavior, eating habits, physical activity levels, risk for obesity, high-risk behaviors, and school performances. These beliefs are in accordance with the preponderance of accumulated research on media's various negative effects on children."[31] But the research team also found pediatricians see parents as the greatest obstacle to their recommending viewing guidelines. The doctors often failed to recommend guidelines during office visits because they believed parents would be unresponsive.

Your pediatrician may be reluctant to tell you, but we aren't. *Don't make the television, or any electronic media for that matter, a substitute for you.* There is no replacement for an engaged parent. Regardless of the quality and intent of the program, it offers no personal interaction—your kid receives no accolades or verbal reinforcement, nor any constructive criticism, from the screen. Your preschooler will not be applauded for completing the alphabet or corrected when missing the number eight when counting to ten. Long hours spent behind the screen is lost time—time you could have used to play with, read to, and strengthen your relationship with your child.

Viewing Recommendations

We agree with the pediatricians' ban on television for children under the age of two. And for children over two, rather than the two-hour limit pediatricians set, we believe one hour a day of television or video is plenty. Make sure the shows your children watch are age-appropriate quality programming. In the next few paragraphs, we provide some ideas.

After your youngster has read a book, you can sometimes find the story on DVD or video at the library. Not only does this encourage reading, but it reinforces comprehension skills. When your child sees the story on video, it can increase his or her understanding of the tale. For example, *Peter Rabbit* or *Frog and Toad Together* both have a DVD or video version that can be watched after reading the books.

A trip to the zoo, museum, or vacation spot can also be

enhanced by selecting a DVD related to the excursion. For example, if your child enjoyed watching the bears at the zoo, you can not only check out books on bears but can also check out a DVD or video about them. If you are planning a visit to Massachusetts, for instance, you might check out a video on the Boston Tea Party.

For older preschoolers, you can incorporate nonfiction video selections into your child's viewing time and enhance his or her overall knowledge. There are some great science video series available, such as *Bill Nye the Science Guy*, *The Magic School Bus*, and *Eyewitness*. These series explore almost every science topic imaginable: Animals, the human body, weather, and space are just a few examples. History and geography subjects are also available in electronic media. Again, the library is often helpful in finding DVDs and videos for all these subjects. If you have cable or satellite television, you may already have access to many of these types of programs.

You may want to include old-time shows or movies in your child's viewing. This programming tends to be simpler, slower paced, and less visually stimulating. These shows can provide a youngster with historical perspective as well. Comedians like Laurel and Hardy, the Three Stooges, and Charley Chaplin are funny to watch, and you can point out differences in the time periods, such as transportation and clothing.

Most importantly, don't forget that video selections should not be a substitute for reading or real-life experiences, but rather a supplement. Again, stick to a one-hour per day limit.

Learning from Computers

Computers have been increasing their presence in American homes over the recent years. In 1984, 8 percent of households had a home computer, and by 2000, over half of homes had them.[32] Many parents believe computers are a necessity for early childhood education. Take a jaunt down the software aisle at a nearby electronics store, and you will discover a varied selection of software programs for the young mind. But does the computer provide the magic bullet for growing a preschooler's mind that many parents think?

Some research suggests preschool-age children can learn skills from computer instruction. For instance, Rosalyn Shute and John Miksad from The Flinders University of South Australia found that when children received instruction from computer software, their language skills, such as word knowledge, improved but their math skills, such as counting and sorting, did not.[33]

Likewise, Feng Din from the University of St. Francis and Josephine Calao from the Newark School District studied five- and six-year-old children and found those who played educational video games gained in spelling and reading skills, but, like Shute and Miksad, the researchers found the children did not show gains in math skills.[34]

On the other hand, researchers from The University of Missouri, Columbia, found children's use of educational software at home was positively correlated with reading and math abilities in kindergarten.[35] But by third grade, the use of educational software was *negatively* associated with reading and math achievement. The researchers hypothesize that the educational software may be a poor fit for children in the later years. The team presented another possible explanation: Those who do more poorly in school may be provided with more educational software. In other words, the use of educational software does not cause poor school performance, but those children who struggle in school may use it more often at home.

While both these explanations are plausible, we have a different conjecture. Some research suggests your preschooler can gain rudimentary skills from using educational software, but we believe learning though software is limited. Researchers from the Bar-Ilan University in Israel studied 150 kindergarten children between ages five and six, from mostly middle-class families.[36] They found children who used computers at home had lower abstract thinking scores than those who did not. The researchers discussed previous studies that showed that when children using software are not guided, they act more impulsively, which may prohibit higher thinking. Children are "more likely to get caught up in trial-and-error processes devoid of conceptualization."

If you watch youngsters use software, you find they are enthralled with the bells and whistles of the programming; they are quickly absorbed by the interactive quality of the experience. Children are often more attentive and less distracted when taking a seat behind the computer screen than when listening to the teacher's instructions.[37] Adults, too, respond similarly. Whether surfing the Web or playing a game, how many times have you sat behind a computer for a few minutes, only to find an hour or more has passed without your realizing it?

If working with software maintains a child's attention better than listening to a teacher, you may conclude that a child should learn more from a computer. But maintaining a child's interest says little of the resulting ability of the child to learn the material. For example, one software program teaches rhyming words. A talking fish in a bowl asks the user to select an item that rhymes with a series of words. The program is certainly entertaining, but just because a child is enthralled by the program does not mean the he or she will increase his or her rhyming skills. It may simply be that watching a talking fish is amusing! And if the child is successful in matching the word, it does not mean he or she has increased phonological awareness; it could be that through trial and error the youngster has remembered the sequence. In fact, some conclude that when children use software rather than focusing on learning the material, the superfluous entertainment becomes the epicenter of the youngster's attention. Unfortunately, this is opposite of the desired effect.[38]

Researchers have found that the more beneficial children's software applies the principle of scaffolding, which means it assesses the ability of the child and gives more difficult exercises as the child becomes more proficient at the task(s).[39] While this may sound impressive, it is a technique that teachers and parents have intuitively applied for generations. For example, when your little one starts with a beginning reader, he or she will encounter a word that's difficult to pronounce. Your instruction adapts to your child's level by helping him or her sound out the word. Next time through the book, your junior reader may not need the additional help, and you will decide he or she is ready to tackle a more difficult book. In this scenario, you have intuitively applied the principle of scaffolding.

If you choose to use educational software, your child will benefit more if you work with your youngster when he or she is using it. In a research paper titled "The Use of Computers in Kindergarten, With or Without Adult Mediation; Effects on Children's Cognitive Performance and Behavior," researchers from the Bar-Ilan University found that those children who had an adult help when using software benefited more than those without any aid beyond technical support.[40]

On the balance, we believe that euphoria over computers as tools for learning is misplaced. And more time on the computer may not be better; in fact, researchers from Wayne State University and The Ohio State University suggest more time may be worse. They found children who were heavy computer users performed worse on IQ tests as well as visual and motor skill evaluations.[41]

In their research conclusions, Shute and Miksad hoped that their work would help "dispel the myth of computers as magical toys, as many parents and early childhood educators believe."[42] Resources are squandered and false hopes nurtured as a result of the illusion that computers serve as a magical tool for children's learning. In addition, parents are anxious to place their children behind a computer to give them a head start on the latest technology, fearful that if he or she is not rapping the keyboard by age three, their child may fall irrecoverably behind their peers. Parents believe their youngsters must acquire computer skills early to prepare them for the future. However, as bestselling author and educational psychologist Jane Healy points out, there is no critical time period for developing computer skills.[43] You can learn at age ten, twenty, or forty—and even older. The preoccupation with preparing a preschooler for tomorrow's job market by getting him or her up to speed today is largely unfounded—because today's technology will shortly become obsolete. Nearly every year, there is new software to learn that replaces the old style and technology.

In the end, we believe that time spent at home on educational software is better spent reading to your child or even playing a board game. Doing such activities with your child will provide better foundations for the later school years.

Choosing Software

If you do choose to use software to supplement your child's education, look for programs that use scaffolding, as we discussed earlier. Make sure any computer software is appropriate for the young and impressionable mind. To help you choose software that is appropriate for a youngster, most children's software games include a rating by the Entertainment Software Rating Board (ESRB) on the package. The ratings are based upon content such as violence, language, sex, gambling, and drugs. Here are is a list of the ratings and the corresponding definitions as defined by the board:

- Early Childhood (EC)
  Titles rated EC (Early Childhood) have content that may be suitable for ages three and older. Contains no material that parents would find inappropriate.
- Everyone (E)
  Titles rated E (Everyone) have content that may be suitable for ages six and older. Titles in this category may contain minimal cartoon, fantasy, or mild violence and/or infrequent use of mild language.
- Everyone 10+ (E 10+)
  Titles rated E 10+ (Everyone 10 and older) have content that may be suitable for ages ten and older. Titles in this category may contain more cartoon, fantasy, or mild violence, mild language and/or minimal suggestive themes.
- Teen (T)
  Titles rated T (Teen) have content that may be suitable for ages thirteen and older. Titles in this category may contain violence, suggestive themes, crude humor, minimal blood, simulated gambling, and/or infrequent use of strong language.
- Mature (M)
  Titles rated M (Mature) have content that may be suitable for ages seventeen and older. Titles in this category may contain intense violence, blood and gore, sexual content, and/or strong language.
- Adults Only (AO)
  Titles rated AO (Adults Only) have content that should only be viewed by persons eighteen and older. Titles in this category may include prolonged scenes of intense violence and/or graphic sexual content or nudity.

- Rating Pending (RP)
  Titles listed as RP (Rating Pending) have been submitted to the ESRB and are awaiting final rating. (This symbol appears only in advertising prior to a game's release).[44]

A word of caution is in order about this rating system, however. Compliance is voluntary, and many do not agree with the ratings assigned by the video gaming industry. When parents were asked if they agreed with the E ratings given to games presumably suitable for children ages three to seven, one-third did not agree.[45] Our advice is to use the ratings for guidance, but take a close look at content. After your youngster breaks open the package and starts to play, look over his or her shoulder to make sure it meets with your approval.

And of course, allow your child to use any software only in moderation, as longer hours are associated with poor grades[46].

Screen Time Sanity

Experts frequently express concern that too much time spent on media, whether television or computers, may sacrifice traditional childhood experiences. Hours behind a television, computer, or video game may replace time for playing with friends in the yard, collecting bugs, or working puzzles. As your authors and as parents, we do not propose a ban on all electronics; at times, they can serve a purpose. Sometimes you must get things done free from the distraction of young ones, and your child may benefit if you choose quality programming, as we suggested earlier.

For the occasions you choose to use this media, the secret to eliminating conflict is to make sure your expectations are clear upfront (otherwise you are likely to hear "just five more minutes!" or worse yet, witness a tantrum). We always tell our sons how long they will be allowed to watch a movie before the film rolls, and we permit no more than thirty to forty-five minutes a day of viewing. Just to make sure they conclude watching their movie without a struggle, we set a timer, and show time ends at the beep. If there is a conflict after the time is up—no movie or computer next time. However, they don't watch every day because they are busy with other things. Likewise, we allow our boys no more than thirty minutes of computer time a couple times a week. The earlier you set the rules, the fewer problems you will have in the future.

We urge a minimalist approach to viewing television or working with software. As a rule, limit movie, computer, and television time. Don't let electronic media become the center of your household. Instead, do the activities we recommend in this book so that your child develops interests in other things and the screen is not so important. In addition, make sure time spent viewing media or being at the computer does not displace other, more enriching activities.

Mozart, Michelangelo, and Shakespeare:

How the Arts Can Shape the Mind

THE BELIEF THAT MUSIC could be beneficial to the intellectual development of children has existed for many years. In fact, the ancient Greeks considered music a branch of mathematics.[1] Intrigued by the relationship between mathematics and music, Gordon Shaw and his colleagues at the University of California at Irvine sought empirical support. Shaw and his colleagues developed a mathematical model that described how neural messages are transmitted in the brain. The model was a spatial-temporal representation of the neurons in the brain that defined the arrangement and firing sequence of the neurons. Out of curiousity, researchers created a program that matched pitches and instruments to the mathematical model—and music emerged. Shaw then hypothesized that listening to music may stimulate the same neurons required for spatial-temporal reasoning, which is the ability to manipulate three-dimensional objects in your mind. The resulting experiment would lead to a landmark discovery known as the "Mozart Effect."

The Mozart Effect

In order to explore a possible relationship between music and the mind, Shaw teamed with Frances Rauscher, herself a concert cellist and clinical psychologist, and colleague Katherine Ky. They chose Mozart's compositions because they believed that since he began composing at the early age of four, he must have drawn upon the brain's innate spatial-temporal ability to do so. The team gathered thirty-six college students and tested their IQs before and after listening to a ten-minute Mozart sonata.[2] Just as the researchers predicted, the students' brain power increased; they gained about nine IQ points on the Visual-Spatial Processing portion of the Stanford-Binet IQ test, but the benefits lasted only about as long as the short sonata played. The resulting brain boost was thereafter dubbed the "Mozart Effect."

Some subsequent research failed to corroborate that listening to music produced higher spatial scores, and this prompted Rauscher and Shaw to review the results.[3] Shaw and Rauscher acknowledged that there were many different types of spatial abilities and that only the spatial-temporal tasks would be impacted. In terms of the other research results, they believed in some cases the tests used did not accurately measure spatial-temporal ability; in other cases, the music had not been structured and complex enough to stimulate the brain.

Still other researchers have developed competing theories

to explain the temporary gains from listening to music. Basically, they hypothesize the enhanced short-term performance of the listener is due to improved mood, or an aroused state, which improves his or her intellectual performance.[4] There are issues with these explanations, however. One is that with arousal, all forms of cognitive tasks should be enhanced—which is not the case here. Another concern is that if positive mood enhances performance, then a sour mood should inhibit performance. This, again, is not the case.

Following Rauscher and Shaw's discovery of temporary spatial gains from listening to music, Lois Hetland from Harvard University compiled studies to determine if there was consistent experimental support.[5] After analyzing thirty-six studies including 2,465 children, she concluded that there was indeed a short-term benefit from listening to music. Like Rauscher and Shaw, she noted spatial-temporal gains.

Spatial-Temporal Gains

After their initial experiment with college-age students, Rauscher and Shaw wanted to see if younger, more plastic minds would realize long-term gains from musical training, beyond short-term gains from just listening.[6] The team chose keyboard instruction because they believed it provided a visual representation of the notes, which would further develop spatial abilities. For example, a student can see there is a half-step between a black key and a white key, as well as hear the difference in the pitch between the notes. The researchers recruited a group of three- and four-year-old kids; some received keyboard lessons, while the remaining youngsters had singing lessons, computer lessons, or no lessons at all. After six months, only those children who had keyboard instruction showed a dramatic increase in spatial abilities. Since the gains lasted more than a day, the researchers concluded, "This study suggests that music training, unlike listening, produces long-term modifications in underlying neural circuitry."

In a later study, Rauscher recruited kindergarten children and placed them in one of two groups: One had group keyboard lessons twenty minutes twice a week, and the control group did not receive the training.[7] After four months of lessons the children were tested and then tested again after eight months of lessons. Like the previous study, the children who had the lessons had gained in spatial-temporal reasoning, and, as you would expect, the children made greater cognitive gains after eight months of lessons than after four months.

Hetland, who compiled the studies of influence from listening to music referred to earlier, also compiled the available experimental studies.[8] She concluded that spatial-temporal performance in preschool and elementary-aged children continue to improve through two years of music instruction.

Mathematics Gains

Because spatial reasoning is so closely related to mathematics, many believe musical instruction will boost mathematical skills as well. But surprisingly, there is a dearth of research on the music instruction/mathematical relationship. Kathryn Vaughn from Boston College used six experimental studies to put together a meta-analysis to determine if children who studied music made gains in mathematics. She determined there was a causal relationship, in that music instruction produces higher math scores. At the same time, she cautioned that since the available evidence was so scarce, she could not confirm the relationship with complete certainty.[9]

Reading Gains

Some studies have examined the relationship between music ability and early pre-reading skills. Sima Anvari and her colleagues at McMaster University in Canada gave one hundred four- and five-year-old children a battery of tests and found that music skills were correlated with phonological awareness and children's reading ability.[10] The children who possessed higher musical skills, such as pitch and rhythm, also had greater phonemic awareness, which includes rhyming and combining letters to make sounds. Also, the youngsters scored higher on letter identification and word comprehension.

While the prior study was correlational, Joyce Gromko from Bowling Green State University provided experimental evidence that children's music instruction could enhance pre-reading skills. She placed kindergarten children into two groups: a test group, in which the youngsters learned songs, had rhythmic training, and were taught music theory over a period of four months; and a control group, which did not receive any music instruction during the same time frame.[11] Both groups had their letter sound knowledge tested before and after the test period. For example, the examiner would give the youngster the word "hat," and then the child would attempt to break the word into its individual letter sounds: "h – a – t." Gromko found the children who received music training performed significantly better on identifying the letter sounds than those who did not receive the training

In another study, Irving Hurwitz and his colleagues found children performed better on a standardized reading test after enrollment in the Kodaly Music Training Program, which uses folk songs to teach music basics.[12] The researchers divided first-grade children with similar IQs and socioeconomic status into two groups. The test group was provided with music training, which focused upon singing for forty minutes a day, five days a week, throughout the school year, while the control group received no music training. By the end of the year, not only did the children who received lessons perform higher on tests of spatial abilities, but they were better readers. The children with the music instruction scored in the 88th percentile on the reading test, while those without music instruction were in the 72nd percentile.

While the research suggests a correlation between music and reading, why this is so is not fully understood. There is some evidence that children who are more adept at identifying pitch can more easily identify word and letter sounds.[13] This would imply music training would aid in reading acquisition. Others believe that the same area in the brain processes both speech and music abilities, and training in music may benefit reading skills as well. Whatever the case, more research needs to be done before we know for certain.

Perfect Pitch

Experts now believe that as there is a critical period of development for language and eyesight, there is also a critical period for developing perfect pitch, which is the ability to identify the exact musical note after hearing it. Researchers believe the upper age limits of this development period are between nine and twelve, and attaining absolute pitch after these years is essentially impossible.[14] Therefore, if you want your child to have absolute pitch, early music training is a must.

But there is likely a genetic component to developing absolute pitch as well, because not all children who start music lessons early attain a perfect ear. In other words, providing music lessons for your child may not ensure that he or she develops perfect pitch.

Music at Home

Now that you have seen that music can fine-tune the mind, you are probably asking where you should begin with your child. The answer: You can begin at home. While experts caution that listening to music alone has not been shown to increase intelligence, it is a good way to introduce your young child to music so he or she can acquire an appreciation for music that may last lifetime. And those who enjoy music at a very young age are more likely to pick up an instrument when they are older. Also, by listening to a variety of music, your child's experience is simply more enriched. We know from our little rodent friends, more enrichment is better—to a point of course.

Begin by playing a variety of music at home and in the car. Here are some suggestions to start with:[15]

- Classical music, Renaissance to twentieth century
- Ethnic music from various cultures
- Contemporary popular music
- Jazz
- Children's music

Much or all of this music can be found on the radio, or you can purchase it for your home collection. With a visit to your local library, you can to pick up additional CDs and tapes to increase your youngster's listening exposure.

There is no need to completely rely on prerecorded material, however. Young children enjoy live versions even more – especially if Mom or Dad is the star performer. Fear not: You don't have to sing opera like Pavarotti or hum Beethoven's Fifth. Familiar children's songs such as the "Itsy Bitsy Spider" or "I'm a Little Teapot" are enthusiastically received by younger preschoolers. And once you have hit on a child's personal favorite, you will likely sing it many, many times over. They love repetition at this age. In our case, it started one Christmas season: We sang "Away in the Manger" as a bedtime song. And we sang that tune nightly before bed for a year and a half before our older son tired of it.

Finally, don't be afraid to improvise. Create new lyrics to an old tune, or create a new song from scratch. Your youngsters will really crack up when you ad-lib lyrics and tunes. Make music wherever you are: at the grocery store, in the bathtub, or driving in the car.

Adding gestures and movement to music gives it a new dimension, too. Again, be creative. (For those who do not have the creative bug, a quick search on the shelves of your local library or bookstore will provide inspiration.) Here is an example of what we did with a tune that was popular for some time at our house:

Five little monkeys (hold up five fingers)
Jumping on the bed (jump up repeatedly. You may want to avoid jumping on the bed, however.)
One fell off and bumped his head (touch your head)
The mama called the doctor and the doctor said (put fist by ear)
"No more monkeys jumping on the bed." (shake finger)

Let your aspiring musician have a try at instruments. Children love making music, even though your refined ear may not find their attempts quite as pleasing. Collect a variety of instruments that are designed for young hands: toy drums, electronic or acoustic piano, or maracas are good choices. An inexpensive way to add to your child's instrument collection is to buy kitchenware such as cups, bowls, pans, and wooden spoons, or give them kitchenware that is being retired from service. Kids will turn your kitchen into an orchestral hall.

Music Classes

For music instruction, we highly recommend group music classes for every child from birth. It is even more important for children if you intend to give them formal instrumental training.

Two fine group programs are available nationwide: Kindermusik and Music Together. Both offer classes designed to nurture early music abilities in a playful environment, taught by trained instructors. Researchers have shown that this time in the classroom, as well out-of-class, music-centered time, boosts the intellect.[16] The programs provide a wonderful opportunity to acquire such music fundamentals as developing a sense of tone and rhythm. Not only do the children sing and add movements to music, but the budding musicians incorporate instruments suited for their age, such as egg shakers or rhythm sticks. One of our group music teachers, who also taught piano to children, said that kids who took the group music classes were better prepared to start piano lessons. She even recommended that some of her piano students who had not taken group music lessons sign up for them.

Kindermusik and Music Together both have CDs available for your youngster to take home and "practice." This gives your youngster more opportunities to enjoy the music and movements they perform during class. When they return home, they can sing, jump, and shout along with their familiar tunes. But don't be alarmed if your child does not participate actively while in class. He or she may be bashful initially, or may even have a different learning style. Rather then an active learner, your child may be a passive or an observational learner. Both of our boys were this way: they simply watched wide-eyed, but participated minimally. It was a different story after we returned home; when we played their music at home, they performed the singing and dancing movements they had observed in class.

Kindermusik offers several classes for newborns through age seven. The children are grouped by age, although a class for youngsters of multiple ages has recently been added. The youngest children are accompanied by a parent, while older children attend the class independently. You can find more details about these classes by visiting www.kindermusik. com.

Whereas Kindermusik divides most classes by age range, Music Together's signature class is with mixed-age children. Here newborns though children age five participate with a parent in singing, moving, chanting, listening, watching, and/or playing instruments. The mixed ages allow children to learn from on another—the younger by watching older, and the older by modeling for the younger. The primary purpose of the class is to establish what they term basic music competence, or the ability to sing in tune and keep a beat. For Music Together classes in your area, go to www.music-together.com.

Finally, the Yamaha School of Music offers courses and lessons designed for preschoolers that include singing and dancing, as well as an introduction to the keyboard. The classes are designed to prepare preschoolers for piano lessons offered for the elementary student. For more information and locations, visit www.yamaha.com, under music instruction.

There may be various group music programs in your area, so check the Internet, phonebook, or local resources for other options. Also, your city parks and recreation department, as well as any local university, may offer other music classes for young children.

Music Lessons

As to when you should start musical training for your youngster, there is no absolute consensus. Many say a child must have an appropriate attention span, fine motor dexterity, and know how to read the alphabet through the letter G. But the Suzuki method uses a different approach. Rather than reading music from a page, students start at young ages and imitate the teacher. To decide what is best for you and your child, contact a professional teacher near you, or go to www. suzukiassociation.org.

The most popular instrument for beginning musicians is the piano. Although adults have a greater range of play due to their hand size, the keyboard is still very approachable for the small hands of the youngest musicians. The piano also provides a great foundation for future study because a student learns the grand staff, which includes both the bass and treble clef. Finally, in music research, the piano has most often been used to improve intellectual gains. Researchers believe this may be because the student not only hears the sounds of the notes but sees the relationship on the keyboard.

The younger you start your child learning music, the better—within reason, of course. Younger children can make more intellectual gains if they begin when they are in the three- to five-year-old range than those who begin study later.[17] And not surprisingly, children who have private lessons show greater intellectual gains than those who have group lessons.[18] The teacher can structure the pace of learning around the individual student, rather than the group as a whole. However, in our experience as parents, many private piano teachers will not give lessons until the child is five, while group instructors provide lessons for children at younger ages. And parents must assess the physical and emotional maturity of the child to determine when their son or daughter is ready, along with the advice of a teacher of their choice.

Visual Arts

While research shows music can make a kid smarter, other art forms such as dance, drama, and visual arts can enhance creativity, independent thinking, and imagination. If you ever watched little artists in action, you'll notice they are also using problem-solving skills and sequential thinking as they work on their masterpieces. An example of an art exercise that enhances problem-solving skills is creating an elephant with Play-Doh or modeling clay. Your child eventually will determine that the best method to shape a trunk or tail is by rolling a piece into a cylinder. Body parts such as the ears require a different method; in this case, your child may realize that flattening a piece may be the best approach.

In addition to inspiring creative work, Play-Doh can be used to teach shapes, letters, objects, and animals by molding the item. Take turns making the items and guessing what they are. (This exercise requires extra imagination for children whose parents are artistically challenged—like us.) The boxed sets of Play-Doh often include tools and accessories for even more entertainment possibilities.

Here are some basic supplies to get you started on your home art projects:

- Colored pencils
- Crayons
- Markers
- Colored construction paper
- Scissors
- Glue
- Stickers
- Glitter
- Paint and brushes
- Butcher paper or similar for painting

- Coloring books
- Chalk and chalkboard
- Play-Doh or modeling clay

Once you have an arsenal of supplies, finding crafts to do is easy. Search the Internet for children's crafts, coloring pages, or art projects. You can find step-by-step craft instructions for preschoolers. Three of our favorite sites are www.crayola.com, www.dltk-kids.com, and www.familyfun.go.com. Register online, and a variety of craft ideas will be deposited in your e-mail box. If you have a subscription to children's magazines, they regularly offer craft ideas in their pages. There are endless books, too, on children's art projects. If you plan your crafts according to the season of the year, or better yet a current holiday, this will provide a richer learning experience for your child.

Drama and Dance

Beyond the visual arts, drama and dance also can provide an enriched environment. For example, your youngster's memory and sequential thinking will improve by remembering the order of the scenes or steps to a song. You can incorporate the benefits of dramatic play by acting out your youngster's favorite storybook characters. For example, you can huff and puff and pretend to blow the house down when you become the wolf in "The Three Little Pigs." When you mimic the characters' voices, facial expressions, and movements, your preschooler's face will light up with delight. Then, switch roles—your child can be the wolf, and you can be the little pig.

Puppet play can help preschoolers develop oral language skills as they use the characters to create voices and stories. Encourage your child to develop a story and create voices when playing with the puppets. You can make the creation of your puppet friends a craft project in and of itself. Start with an old pair of tube socks and color them with markers. Then, for a decorative touch, add plastic eyes, yarn, and buttons. A simple stage can be created using a shoebox or other cardboard box; decorate it with crayons or markers. If you do not have enough time to create something yourself, you can purchase complete puppet sets that provide the puppets along with a stage for a reasonable price.

Art classes can add a new dimension to your youngster's art experience. Your child gets the expertise of an instructor, uses supplies that may not be readily available at home, and can participate with peers in a group setting. Your child will often return home with projects you never would have thought of. For example, recently our son presented us with a painting that was created with bubble wrap!

Some popular art classes available in our area are: Kidz Kraftz, where kids and parents make unique craft projects; Creative Tots, where children incorporate drama, dance, music, and visual arts with playtime; and Meet the Masters: preschoolers incorporate the ideas and techniques of famous artists into their own work. For classes in your area, check with your local city parks and recreation department, local museums and libraries, community art centers, YMCA, arts and craft stores, or local university.

Preschool-age children love to explore their creative abilities. And as parents, it is easy to incorporate creative art into your week. You can invite a few of your child's friends to share an afternoon of finger painting or puppet theater, or you may enroll your son or daughter in an interesting class. Time spent engaged in any type of creative art will give your youngster an appreciation of the fine arts—and an added brain boost.

On the Home Front:

Promoting Learning through Your Everyday Routines

ARE YOU OFTEN TOO BUSY with tasks at home to spend the time you would like with your child? If so, you are not alone. But with a bit of creativity, much of your work around the house can be transformed into learning time with your youngster. You can use your work to develop problem-solving skills, mathematical and categorizing abilities, and planning, sequencing, and motor skills.

Many basic chores provide opportunities for learning about counting, shape recognition, and classifying. Your housework may take longer with the extra "help," but when you use real world examples, your preschooler can develop basic math concepts that can provide an edge when he or she is ready to start school.

In this chapter, we will show you how to transform common, everyday routines and chores into excellent learning opportunities for your children. Of course, use discretion when working with your child. Allow only the use of tools and utensils that are safe for your preschooler.

Laundry

When helping with laundry, your youngster can learn to sort items or practice math skills such as understanding opposites, counting, and classifying. To teach opposites, let your youngster empty the hamper and place the dark clothing in one pile and the light in another. You can show your helper that the clothes are wet when they come out of the washer and dry when they have completed their cycle in the dryer. Your child can separate items by type: towels, socks, shirts, or group into pairs. Another option is to sort the clothes by family member: one pile for Mom, one for Dad, and one for each sibling. When your child is older, you can ask for help separating the dirty clothing into piles by type of wash cycle: delicate, permanent press, or regular.

Cooking

Time in the kitchen can be useful to teach math skills such as counting, ordinal numbers (i.e. first, second, third...), comparisons, measurement, and fractions. Whether you are making a weekday dinner or a delicious treat, you can incorporate learning while you cook. The key to making sure you turn the cooking process into a learning experience, though, is to adapt the instructions and participation level to your little one.

Here is how we as parents (and bakers!) make chocolate chip cookies with extra "hands." Start by counting; i.e., "one, two, and three eggs." With an older preschooler you might count up the one hundred or so chocolate chips. Show your child the order of ingredients as you put them in the bowl: "First add flour, second sugar, third baking powder, fourth vanilla, and fifth eggs." Compare the amounts of ingredients in the bowl. For example, there is more flour than baking powder. Use your measuring cups and spoons to show relationships between units of volume. You might say, "We need one cup of sugar, which is the same as two one-half cups." Once you have finished making the baked good(s), you can explain fractions: divide a cookie in half, or in quarters. Bon appétit!

Mail and Bills

The last one to our family mailbox may be a rotten egg, a chicken bone, or any other undesirable item. This playfulness adds fun to the mail's arrival and continues as we sort through the envelopes and advertisements; we identify numbers, letters, and the first letter of items we find in catalogues or magazines.

It's also fun for kids to page through the flyers and catalogues to make suggestions for gifts to buy for others. We encourage our boys to circle and place a family member's initials by the items that mom, dad, or brother may want for a birthday or other special days. And even though it may not be the gift we ultimately choose, the selection process encourages them to think critically about what another person may want.

If your family clips coupons, you can use this time to teach your youngster about money and math by showing the different prices on the coupon and comparing the relative costs. You can have your child help find the products you need, then have him or her clip the coupons (with his or her scissors, of course) and sort and, finally, file them.

Bills are no laughing matter, at least for most parents. But you can turn paying the bills into a learning experience for your young one. Start by placing the bills together and explain what each service provides. Describe how payment works: The check is filled out in exchange for a service, then sent to the company. The money is then transferred from your account to the company providing the service. If you have some old checks, let your youngster write some. You can have your child help stuff the envelopes, affix the stamps and labels, and then put them in the mailbox. Explain how the letter goes from your house to the post office for sorting and is then delivered to the business. (If you go online to pay bills, you will have to do a little improvising.)

Chores for Your Preschooler

Assigning your child chores can help develop his or her planning skills and sequential thinking. As a bonus, chores develop responsibility, discipline, and a sense of accomplishment. When each individual's chore contributes to the well-being of the family, children are more likely to help. And in the longer term, having familial chores will also foster individual initiative. Make sure the chores are appropriate for the age and maturity level of each child, however. With a younger preschooler, for example, you may want to guide the planning effort: "In order to clean your room, we must first pick up the big stuffed animals. When we are finished, we will pick up the cars." Some appropriate chores for preschool-aged children may include the following:

- Pick up toys
- Put clothes in hamper
- Set napkins
- Feed the pet

- Dump small bathroom waste basket into larger basket
- Set silverware
- Vacuum with mini vacuum
- Clear table
- Make own bed
- Bring in the groceries
- Water the plants

If it is difficult for your youngster to complete the chores alone, help your son or daughter finish them. As an incentive, you may create a chart of the responsibilities and offer a small reward at the end of the day or week. Rewards need not be monetary but instead could include a game with a parent, extra story time, or, for a job especially well done, a trip to an ice cream shop.

Home Projects

Special projects that you work on with your child at home can help your preschooler develop a wide range of skills: increased vocabulary and knowledge, mathematical and problem-solving skills, and fine and gross motor skills. They teach your child how to approach a problem, devise a solution, and implement a resolution. Whether you are repairing your car or undertaking a woodworking task, try to elicit your youngster's help.

Regardless of the endeavor, the process is similar. Begin with a general description of the problem or the task, then devise solutions; finally, with your child's help, complete the project. During your joint effort, your youngster may slow your progress by losing a tool or asking questions. Be patient and take the extra time—you are developing your relationship as well as your child's young mind. Give your preschooler simple tasks, such as handing you a tool or removing a screw. Explain the purpose of the tools you are using as well as hardware or parts you install. If you have the extra time, you may take out tools that are not required for the task and demonstrate how to use them. Count, measure, add, and subtract, all with the help of your little one.

If your project is not safe for little hands, prepare a separate area for your child to work. If appropriate, your youngster may use some of your hand tools to work on his or her project. You can always set up an area with toy tools as you work alongside, as well. Our son has his workbench set up in the living room, so his tools are always convenient. Generally both boys receive a scrap of wood or other material to work on, or a paintbrush with water. Their task is inevitably finished first (with not as many trips to Home Depot).

Outdoor Projects

Gardening can be a great learning experience for a preschooler. As with most other work, gardening can be a time to teach many skills, such as counting, measuring, and sorting. In addition to these benefits, gardening provides a great opportunity for a science lesson: with seed, water, air, and sun, we can grow a new plant.

Start with a description of each plant in your garden: a flower, leafy vegetable, root vegetable, or bean. Explain the growth timetable for each plant, the uses for the plant, and how deep and far apart to plant the seeds. Discuss the care that will be required, such as the amount of water and fertilizer or pesticides.

Depending upon your climate, you may also have your child help you rake leaves or shovel snow. Then practice counting skills by counting the piles. Or compare relative sizes while you make different sized mounds. If you have snow in your region, you might make a snowman. Not only will you have fun, but deciding which accessories the snowman needs will develop your child's planning abilities.

Family Dinner

One of the best times to build family relationships has traditionally been at the dinner table. Unfortunately, for many families today, dinner is nothing more than grabbing carryout food from the restaurant around the corner and retreating to the TV room or in front of a monitor. Even families eating at the same table are often engaged by the nearby television—nearly six out of ten families eat dinner with the television running.[1] This means that most families in America listen to the television in lieu of dinner conversation; at best, television is a continual distraction.

Even families eating at the same table frequently are disengaged. We were recently eating at a local Italian restaurant, and a family of four sat at a table next to us. The two children, one about three and the other six, immediately fired up their laptops, inserted a DVD, and put on their headphones. Rather than conversing with the family, they sat at the table entranced by the movie the entire meal.

Instead, establish dinner as unobstructed family time. A study conducted by the National Center on Addiction and Substance Abuse at Columbia University found one of the best ways to improve your child's school grades is shared family dinners: Teenagers who ate with their families at least five times a week earned higher academic scores. The kids also had stronger family relationships, with lower incidences of substance abuse.[2]

Although our book is about the preschool-age child rather than the teenager, we can extrapolate these findings. The family dinner creates an ideal environment for intellectual exercise. And a loving family encourages a child to share both ideas and daily experiences.

Mealtimes provide opportunity for families to share each other's day or discuss current events. In our home, dinners always consist of lively conversation. The boys are always anxious to share their day's experience. At times, they are sometimes a little too anxious; it can be difficult for the two of us to have an adult conversation. Still, we engage both boys, asking questions appropriate for their age and comprehension levels. You can talk about what you did at work, current events, or whatever topic will interests your children, because, as you recall from Chapter 5, conversation prepares the groundwork for later reading and academic success.

Here are some examples of dinnertime conversation:

Tell your dad what we did today. Let's talk about the park,
   class, games we did together.
What toys did you play with?
What did you like doing today? What did you not like?
I heard on the news… What do you think about that?
Did you see your friend today? What did you do together?

If you have multiple children, make sure each gets equal time to ask and answer questions or to engage in the conversation, free from any older sibling's interjections.

Bedtime

Can I have a drink of water?
I need to go to the bathroom.
My blanket fell off.
Can I have another song or story?

Any of these bedtime requests sound familiar? Likely so. Most of America's preschoolers seem to read from the same script, and at times it seems like the bedtime curtain will never fall. You can help bring closure by reviewing some of the day's events and planning for tomorrow. In addition to taming your little monsters, this will assist in developing their sequential and critical thinking skills. Here are some ideas:

> *That was an interesting story we read today. Do you remember what happened?*
>
> *I think we will stay home tomorrow. We could get up and read some books and then have breakfast. After breakfast, we can play with your train set.*
>
> *We need to get several things done tomorrow: go to the grocery store, dry cleaner, and bank. Which should we do first, second, and third?*
>
> *We don't have any plans tomorrow. What would you like to do?*
>
> *Tomorrow we will go to the park. First, we will pick up the lemonade and put it in our cooler. Then we will go to the park. And since it is supposed to be hot tomorrow, after the park we will go swimming.*

Be creative and patient at bedtime, as well as throughout the day. Not only can this time spent together be fun, but it can develop thinking skills your youngster will carry into the school years and beyond.

Out and About:

Engaging Your Youngster's Mind While Doing Errands

W E TALKED ABOUT transforming mundane tasks at home into rich learning opportunities; you can do the same with errands. You can teach your child to follow directions, develop planning and problem-solving skills, and learn to categorize, as well as increase overall knowledge, while on the run. You may even enjoy your errands more when they become time for exploration and education.

Drive Time

As we discussed in Chapter 8, exposure to a variety of music is great for the budding mind. It teaches a youngster to discern different rhythms, tones, and instruments. And what better time to do so than in the car! Variety, as they say, is the spice of life, so if you usually listen to pop stations, try out country or classical. You can also bring along favorite CDs or tapes for more musical selections.

Don't forget talk radio. In this forum, the host will present a topic and ask listeners to call in with questions or comments. A brief survey across the AM dial will lead to a plethora of topics: fitness, sports, and gardening are just a few examples. The topics presented can often lead to a discussion with your child. Of course, carefully choose your subjects so you do not expose your child to inappropriate material or language.

As you drive, use the scenery as teaching aids. Here are some examples:

- Colors
  Let's find two items that are green.
  Can you find something yellow?
- Shapes
  Can you help me find a sign shaped like a triangle? Rectangle? Circle?
- Numbers
  I need to find house number 246. That is a 2, a 4, and a 6. Can you locate the house?
- Letters
  I need help finding an address. Can you find Main Street? It starts with "m."
- Directions
  We are going to make a left turn at the light, then a right into the parking lot.
- Critical thinking skills
  Oh, there is some construction. It looks like a new building. What do you think it will be?

■ Inference
*Look, there is a pizza restaurant next to the bowling alley.
That is a good idea. People will probably be hungry after
bowling.*

Car trips can be a boon for family time. Odysseys across
the country provide an opportunity to interact with one another (when siblings are not fighting, of course). When we
were children, we spent hours in the car playing counting
games in which everyone counted blue cars or red barns, or
we sang rounds of the song, "Row, Row, Row Your Boat." By
contrast, many children today routinely sit in the back seat of
their SUV or minivan spellbound by the latest movie showing on a factory-installed drop-down screen. Not quite the
bonding and growth experience of family car games...

So, the next time your family takes a road trip, refrain from
watching movies, or at least reduce the time spent watching
them. Here are some other suggestions to keep your kids actively engaged:

■ Listen to music or talk radio
■ Listen to books on tape
■ Bring travel-size games or cards
■ Play car games such as finding a certain color of car or
looking for letters
■ Bring books for children to read or for parents to read
aloud
■ Bring activity books, pencils, stickers, and crayons
■ Sing together
■ Have a conversation
■ Bring toys

Grocery Shopping

As with driving trips, jaunts to the grocery store can teach preschool concepts.

- Colors
  What color are these bananas?
  Pick out some red apples.
- Numbers
  Pick out four oranges and put them in a sack.
  How many eggs are in a dozen?
  Let's see if you can find the number 2 on any signs in this aisle.
- Money
  You can explain how one item may cost more than another by comparing prices and identifying the more or least expensive one.
  Let's see which carton of milk is more expensive. This one costs $3.00 and this one costs $2.00. Which one costs more?
- Weights
  Use the scales in the produce section to discover that different fruits and vegetables have varying weights and costs; encourage your child to guess which items weigh more.
- Letters
  As you push your cart down the aisles, use the many signs to teach the letters of the alphabet.
  I am looking for a can of tomatoes. "Tomato" starts with the letter "t." Can you help find the tomatoes?
  You can teach the sounds of letters by identifying the first letter of an item by its sound.
  This is butter. It starts with the letter "b" and makes the "buh" sound.

Children will find grocery shopping more fun if you choose a letter of the day and have a treasure hunt to find items that start with the letter. Then, for a reward, you eat some of your bounty later. For example on an "A" day, you can buy apples, asparagus, and almonds. Then for a snack, serve the apples and almonds, and, providing your child will eat asparagus, have that vegetable with dinner.

Fitness Center

Many parents belong to fitness centers. And while the quality of the equipment and variety of classes is a primary concern when joining a heath club, you should also consider the availability of childcare. Health clubs generally offer childcare either for free or a nominal charge. Childcare facilities can range from a small space with a TV and a couple toys to multi-room care centers. They may include basketball courts, climbing structures, playgrounds, and computers. Often the childcare workers plan activities, such as crafts. The facility that provides the most for the child is not necessarily more expensive than another that provides minimal services.

As you tour the childcare center, notice if there is a television running at all times. Your preschooler may end up parked in front of it, rather than enjoying other activities. Are educational products available, such as puzzles, games, and books? Are a large quantity and variety of toys easily accessible? Is there a playground so that your child gets some exercise? Is there a high staff-member-to-child ratio so your kid gets individual attention? Ask if there are planned activities for the kids, such as story time or crafts.

Differences between gyms can be striking, even those under the same name. We belong to one YMCA where there is both an outdoor and indoor climbing structure for the children. The facility is huge, with lots of toys, puzzles, games, and books. The staff oversees a daily activity or craft designed to develop the youngster's skills.

At one time, our regular YMCA was being remodeled, and we went to another nearby YMCA. The available childcare there was terrible. Far from the sprawling climbing structures, the care center was contained in a small room with no play equipment whatsoever. Rather than offering a daily craft, the employee sat disengaged, with the television running non-stop.

Activity Bag

Make your educational tools portable by creating an activity bag. Start with a book bag or backpack and fill it with books, notebooks, crayons, pencils, coloring books, activity books, travel games, and cards. Activity bags are useful not only on long trips, but also around town when waiting for appointments or at restaurants before your food arrives. With an activity bag, your child will always have a fun and educational resource available. For an extra special activity, make a book bag with your preschooler. You can buy a blank canvas book bag at a craft store to decorate with fabric paint, glitter, or sequins; personalize it with his or her name.

While bringing an activity bag can certainly help engage your child, the key is to creatively use whatever is around you. Whether you are shopping at your local grocery store or traveling in your car, use your time together as an opportunity for learning, and, of course, fun.

Healthy Body, Healthy Mind:

Exercise and Nutrition

A BOOK ON COGNITIVE DEVELOPMENT would not be complete without addressing exercise and nutrition. And a casual observation of today's youth is enough to cause concern: As many as 20 percent of children ages two to five are at risk for being overweight, and only one in five meet the USDA's guideline of eating five vegetable servings a day.[1] (This statistic even includes French fries, which are one-quarter of the vegetables consumed—hardly a nutritionist's dream!) At the same time, exercising outdoors has dropped off, particularly in urban areas, where people are more transient and fewer children make lifelong neighborhood friends. Instead of playing kickball in the cul-de-sac or hide and seek in the backyard, youngsters rely on electronic games for entertainment. We all know that a healthy diet and exercise can lead to a healthier heart, appropriate weight, and a reduced chance of diabetes. But can nutritious foods and physical activity also increase intelligence and academic performance?

Yes, and no. Aside from malnutrition, most studies do not find that diet has an impact on IQ. However, malnutrition, or a severe deficiency of key vitamins and minerals, has been shown to have long-term negative effects on cognitive ability. Researchers followed 1,385 children from the ages three through eleven from the island of Mauritius, which is off the coast of Africa.[2] They found that the boys and girls who were malnourished at the age of three tested lower on IQ tests and reading ability and demonstrated lower academic performance.

If you are reading this book, it is quite unlikely that your child falls under this category; you are a concerned parent, and therefore your child is probably eating regularly under your watch. But as every parent knows, children will perform their best when they are given quality food to nourish their brains and bodies.

USDA Recommended Daily Food Allowance

The Center for Nutrition Policy and Promotion, which is an organization within the United States Department of Agriculture, offers colorful, kid-friendly illustrations and activities that describe the recommended servings for children.[3] Go to www.mypyramid.gov to learn how you can tailor food servings based upon the age, gender, and activity level of your child. For example, here are the daily recommended servings for a four-year-old boy who is physically active more than sixty minutes a day (which they also recommend):

- Five ounces of grains (half of which should be whole grains)
- Two cups of vegetables
- 1.5 cups of fruits (go easy on sugary juices)
- Two cups of milk products (low-fat or fat-free)
- Five ounces of meat and beans (low-fat or lean meats and poultry; choose more fish, beans, peas, nuts, and seeds)
- Five teaspoons of oils
- Limit extras, such as solid fats and sugars, to 130 calories a day

Nutrition

With young kids around, we know it is not easy to plan healthful meals and snacks and then get your children to eat that way. But you establish your child's eating habits for life early—either good or bad. Like most things worthwhile, it is difficult at first. But if you are persistent and creative, you can "create" a youngster who will eat healthy meals—and may even enjoy them!

Make sure you review the ingredients on food labels to ensure that your child is getting proper nutrition. It is easy to be fooled into thinking you are choosing something healthy. For example, many people will choose juice as a healthy alternative to soda. But when selecting juice it is important to choose 100 percent juice and not those with only 10 percent juice. Beware of the varieties that say "made with real fruit juice" or "all natural." Upon closer observation, you'll see that they may contain little real fruit juice. Usually there is only 10 percent real fruit juice; the rest is good ole sugar water—or rather, high fructose corn syrup. And the "all natural" can mean all natural sugar water. Manufacturers such as Nestle Juicy Juice or Capri Sun offer 100 percent juice options.

When reading food labels, remember the ingredients are listed in order of prevalence in the food. If the first couple of ingredients consist of sugar or high fructose corn syrup, you may want to pass. Also avoid foods that are high in sodium or trans fats. It is important not to confuse trans fats with the omega 3 fats found in fish. Omega 3 fats have been found to be fine brain food, providing great neurotransmission, or passing of information between brain cells. In fact, for the older brain, fish consumption has been shown to reduce the risk of dementia by 60 percent and Alzheimer's disease by 70 percent.[4] On the other hand, trans fats such as those found in fried foods should be avoided, as they are a culprit in heart disease.

If your youngster twists your arm to purchase a box of whatchama-call-its, with the latest cartoon character poised and ready for action on your journey through the supermarket aisles, make sure it is something you want your child to eat. If not—resist! Food companies make a fortune selling junk food by associating it with a favorite character. Lastly, your health food store has many additional great foods that often are not available through you local grocer. Many food products now use alternatives to refined sugars as sweeteners. Cereals, for example, may use fruit juices as sweeteners, rather than refined sugars.

As a parent, you may want to get some books on children's nutrition to further assist you in making good food choices for your family. You can also encourage your kids to understand the basics of nutrition by getting some children's books on the topic. Additionally, there are some kid-friendly cookbooks available, with fun recipes designed for kids to prepare.

Healthy Eating Suggestions

Make sure there are plenty of nutritious food choices in your house. Every child has unique tastes, and hopefully you will discover healthy foods your kids enjoy. Novel foods such as shelled sunflower seeds, mangos, papayas, cashew butter, or veggie chips are tasty and fun, yet packed with nutrients. (If you have younger children, make sure seeds, nuts, and raisins do not pose a choking hazard.) Dips, too, add more excitement to fruits and vegetables; experiment with apples dipped in yogurt, or carrots with hummus. Making fruit smoothies or popsicles is a great way to sneak more fruit into the little one's diet, and doing so is a family event in our house. After we fill the blender with frozen fruit, yogurt, and a banana for good measure, the entertainment begins with the whir of the motor as our kids shout out, "The Smoothie Show, the Smoothie Show!" When the show is over, we divide the spoils. Our boys love it.

Elicit your child's help when you prepare snacks or meals. Children can spread peanut butter on crackers with a plastic knife, place food items onto a plate, or mix ingredients. Helping with the preparation makes it more fun, at least for the younger chef. A child is more likely to finish the meal or to give more novel foods a try if he or she had a hand in the preparation.

Try to schedule consistent meal and snack times in your home to encourage self-control in eating. Also, make sure your child eats at the table, which helps limit nibbling during unplanned meal times. If children get into the habit of eating whenever they desire, they develop poor eating habits and less self-control.

Dinner can be an enjoyable time to catch up on the day's events, while providing your kids with the daily nutrition their growing brains and bodies require. But it can also be a trying time for parents, because you will likely have an occasional dietary struggle. Our dinnertime secret weapon is dessert. Many preschoolers will gobble vegetables if they know a healthy treat is waiting at the end of the meal. In order for this strategy to be effective, never give in to tearful pleas. We have learned the hard way not to make bargains; negotiations to finish the broccoli *after* the ice cream are a big mistake. Try to refrain from serving dessert laden with empty calories, too. Instead, frozen yogurt, fruit smoothies, juice popsicles, or healthy cookies are good alternatives.

When preparing dinner for the family, try to fix a well-balanced meal, based upon the USDA Recommended Daily Allowance, without providing a special menu (unless your child has special dietary needs such as food allergies). It may take some work, but as a rule, our kids eat what we eat. There are exceptions, of course. You may have a craving for a particularly spicy or exotic dish that your kids just will not eat—despite the prize at the end of the meal. Or you may not want to give them expensive sea bass when grilled chicken will do the job. In the end, if your kids eat what you eat, you will create a less picky eater and make meal preparation easier.

Finally, like all behavior, the best way to show is to do. In other words, be a good role model. Your child will want to eat what you eat. Unfortunately, the opposite is also true. It is less convincing for Renee to tell our boys they cannot have soda when she is drinking her diet soda. Our older child will put forth the challenge, *"Why do you get it?"*

Eating Out

Outings go hand in hand with snacks. Whether you're going to the park, on a road trip, or to a museum, quests lose their magic without a tasty companion available. But snacks not need be synonymous with poor eating habits. In fact, choosing the *right* snack can "do your child's body good," as they say. Rather than unhealthy snack fare such as candy and chips, you can fill your snack bag with goodies such as raisins, nuts, wheat crackers, or granola. Or if you want to take a more convenient route, grab prepackaged alternatives. There are many choices, from trail mixes to granola bars. Our kids like the small boxes of raisins, as well juice boxes, which are a great alternative to sodas.

Bring your bag of snacks with on your trips to supply an alternative to eating in restaurants. We almost always pack a lunch when we go to the park or zoo, or for any other outdoor activity. It is fun for the kids to eat their lunch on a picnic blanket or on a bench overlooking a lake—and cheaper than eating out. When we meet our playgroup, each family brings a food item or drink to share with the group. It is exciting for the kids to try their friend's treats and easier for each parent to pack one type of food or drink. Keep a small cooler or travel bag handy to keep the food cool and more appealing. When you bring your own food, it should be easy to surpass the kids' lunches served up at most eateries, as the gold standard for kids is generally chicken fingers with French fries or some variation. Not so healthy!

If you do eat at a restaurant for lunch, soup and salad buffets are great choices because they offer healthy food at a reasonable price. If you have a picky eater, buffets provide a large selection and may offer frozen yogurt, which youngsters may enjoy eating after finishing the healthy stuff. If you by chance do end up at a fast food restaurant, most have healthy sides you can add to your child's main course: milk, juice, fruit, yogurt, and salad are common alternatives.

Exercise

Studies have shown exercise can boost the brain. For instance, the Salk Institute in La Jolla, California, separated genetically identical mice into two groups: One was given only food and water, and another was given access to a running wheel along with food and water.[5] The mice with the running wheel ran an average of three miles a night. After six weeks, the researchers found these mice not only had fitter bodies but better brains than their sedentary cage mates. Those who passed the time running were able to navigate mazes more efficiently. When the brains of the two groups of mice were further examined, those mice that exercised had even created new neurons!

While the brain-boosting benefits of exercise still need more research, there are some time-tested approaches where children can make physical and emotional gains. Sports offer a great environment in which children learn social skills such as good sportsmanship and teamwork. Additionally, in this supervised environment, they have the latitude to physically act out in a controlled and socially acceptable manner without academic pressure. The kids receive instruction in a semiformal setting and then practice what they learned.

Some of the more popular team sports for preschoolers include soccer, t-ball, and basketball. These group sports are well suited for younger children because they have simple rules, require only basic strategy, and improve gross motor skills. These sports also teach children to work as a team.

Soccer is a good team sport to start your preschooler with. It is appealing to younger athletes because it is a fast-moving game, and most preschoolers love to run and kick a ball. It is also a good starter sport because the entry level skills are minimal, but at the same time it takes years to master. You will find youngsters start the soccer season by clustering around the ball, kicking wildly. Over time, the cluster size shrinks; by the end of the season you might even see a child pass to another teammate.

Because soccer focuses on basic motor skills, it provides a great foundation for your child's later athletic ventures. One friend of ours has coached elementary boys in basketball for many years and found that the youngsters who spent time on the soccer field stood out from their peers. On the balance, the kids with prior soccer experience had better foot work than those who did not play.

Individual sports are also good for children because they emphasize concentration and self-control, as well as practicing motor skills. In addition to social and motor skill development, a youngster strives for a personal best or a greater mastery of the sport. For example, achieving the next belt level in karate is great for building a child's self-esteem and self-discipline; he or she has accomplished something on his or her own merit and can be very proud of this. Creating a positive image of oneself, as well as developing self-discipline, will serve a youngster well as a student, and throughout life. Other suitable individual sports choices for preschoolers include gymnastics and swimming.

We believe organized sports can be good for older preschoolers as long as parents do *not* put pressure on the child to perform but instead emphasize the importance of effort, teamwork, and good sportsmanship. While there is no hard and fast rule to determine when your child is ready, it is hard to justify placing a three-year-old in an intense sports program. Of course you are the best person to determine when your youngster is ready, based upon both physical and emotional development. We started our oldest son at age five, and even as the year passed, we could see him mature both physically and emotionally. This was particularly noticeable in his (and his teammates') ability to pay attention. In the beginning of the season, some of the kids were more interested in capturing an imaginary villain in the backfield than pursuing the ball. And occasionally a disinterested youngster would even wander off during drills or take a seat in the field during game play. This changed for nearly all the aspiring athletes as the season progressed. As long as your youngster is not a discipline problem for the coach, be patient, and enjoy the show.

You can find inexpensive sports opportunities for your child through city parks and recreation departments or at your local YMCA. Private leagues, clubs, and studios also offer sports and classes with highly trained coaches and instructors, for more money. For the most part, we do not feel this is money well spent. The increased expectations and pressure to perform at a young age may cause more harm than good, and some child experts express concern when too much pressure is placed on a youngster to perform too early.

To be sure, some parents can have high expectations for their child—too high. They often think they have a little Tiger Woods or Michael Jordan on their hands. Over-emphasizing your preschooler's athletic talents may destroy the child's spirit if he or she feels parental expectations are not being met.

We saw trouble ahead for one young boy on our son's YMCA soccer team. The five-year-old was clearly a gifted soccer player, but you could see his parents' pressure to perform mount as the season wore on. After meeting his dad, you better understood one source of the ambition; the father himself had played in college and was currently active in local leagues. The aspiring young athlete wanted to make his dad proud. You could see the stress the child was under when another player managed to score against him; the boy was devastated. He would cry until consoled by his mother or other teammates. At the end of the season, his mother informed us he would not be returning to play with the YMCA. Instead, he was being enrolled in a private league. The mom said she planned to place her son in a more competitive league where they would help him earn a college scholarship. This boy was only *five*! We knew this little guy had some tough times ahead, and we doubted whether he was ready for more competition, since already he was showing he could not handle the competition in the "lesser" league.

A couple lessons can be learned here. First, keep things in perspective—let your child enjoy his or her childhood. There will be plenty of years ahead that include pressure to perform; why start at age five? And secondly, make sure they are his or her *own* goals. This is true whether your child is five or fifteen. As parents, we let our son choose any sport he wants, as long as our schedule permits. He always has the option of *not* playing a sport; he controls his own athletic path.

Keeping those ideas in mind, here are suggestions for youth sports:

- City parks and recreation departments
- www.ymca.net
- www.thelittlegym.com
- www.gymboreeclasses.com

But when it comes to exercise for your preschool-aged child, outdoor free play cannot be beat, not only for exercise, but for the whole host of reasons we gave in Chapter 6. If you decide it is right for your child to participate in organized sports, do not eliminate the outdoor fun. Many of the benefits of sports can be replicated by simply setting up soccer goals or a baseball diamond in your backyard. We spend many hours together with our boys kicking the soccer ball though makeshift goals behind the house. In this way we are able to incorporate the whole family into the action, which is difficult to do in an organized sport.

Whichever form of exercise you choose for your youngster, make sure your son or daughter gets plenty of daily physical activity. At this age, they have more than enough energy to go around, and as a parent, you need to make sure some of it is expended running, jumping, and playing every day, while you provide their young bodies with nutritious meals and snacks.

Around Town:
Community Resources

I T IS NOT NECESSARY to break the proverbial piggy bank to provide an enriched environment for your child. Many resources can be found in your local community for free or at a reasonable price. What is available to you, of course, will vary depending upon where you live, but options can be found if you keep your eyes open. Larger cities may offer more zoos and museums, while smaller towns may allow greater access to nature. Sometimes less populous areas require a bit more effort, but with some imagination, you will find there is plenty around you to stimulate your youngster.

Local Businesses

Local businesses often offer free or inexpensive educational opportunities in the hope of generating future business. For example, bookstores may host free weekly story times; home supply stores often offer free classes, with such topics as making a wooden birdhouse; and arts and craft stores generally provide a variety of workshops. Local businesses such as ice cream or doughnut shops sometimes sponsor tours—they may even give a free sample!

Nonprofit

Your city library frequently provides educational opportunities, including story time, crafts, or special presentations designed for the young mind. For example, our city library offers a preschool story time with songs and puppets. Most libraries will also offer a list of suggested books geared for your child's developmental level. The local YMCA, as well as your city parks and recreation department, sponsor a wide range of inexpensive classes, with financial assistance often available for those who qualify.

Zoo and Park Visits

Preschoolers have an innate interest in animals, so take the time to foster their curiosity and teach them about animals. If there is a zoo in your area, make frequent visits. Check out family memberships. If you go more than three times a year, it is usually more cost-effective to become a member. Not only will you save money, but you are likely to go more often. To find zoos in your area, or to locate them before you vacation, check out www.zoos-worldwide.de for information.

After you arrive at the zoo, engage your child while you tour. Talk about the animals' physical characteristics, habitat, and behavior. For example, when you see a giraffe eating from a tree, you might point out that the animal's long neck helps the giraffe reach the tall trees. Or, as you look at a reptile display, you might note that the animal's green color matches the green leaves of its habitat, which helps it hide from predators and survive in the wild.

If you do not have a nearby zoo, keep in mind that every city has parks. Larger parks or reserves are home to ducks, birds, fish, butterflies, and other animals that young children enjoy seeing in their natural environments. If you are fortunate enough to live near an aquarium, your kid can learn about sea animals. In addition, nearly every city, regardless of the size, has a pet store. So as Puffy's bag of food nears empty, stop in for a quick tour. This may not be the safari you dreamed of, but it is convenient for you and fun for your child to see the animals on display. And the voyage is free (not counting Puffy's bag of food, of course!).

Museums

Museums provide in-depth presentations of subjects that are usually grouped by themes, such as science, history, and transportation. The great thing about museums is, unlike the adult "been-there-done-that" attitude, for a child every trip is a new experience. With each subsequent trip, your preschooler brings a more developed brain. As a result, your child can take away something different every time he or she visits. For example, we have a pioneer village near our home with a frontier house on display; here is an example of how you might tailor such an experience to your child's developmental level.

- To a three-year-old, you might say:
  This is the house the pioneers lived in. There is a door and many windows. Let's count the windows: 1, 2, 3, 4. There are four windows.
- To a four-year-old, you might say:
  This house is much smaller than our house. It is made of wood, and our house is made of brick.

- To a five-year-old, you might say:
  Look at the big doors and windows. There were no air conditioners back then, so they needed to cool the house by letting the evening air in through the larger doors and windows.

Museums appeal to multiple senses, making them engaging so learning is easier for children. The displays provide a visual component to concretely demonstrate abstract concepts that the young mind does not yet grasp. For example, you can read to your child about the twenty-foot-tall Tyrannosaurus Rex. But when a full-sized replica of the dinosaur is towering above, the youngster begins to understand what twenty feet really means. Because your child can feel the bumps on a meteorite or the ridges of a fossil replica, museums appeal to the sense of touch too.

Some museums are dedicated entirely to children, while others may contain a section for them. The Arizona Youth Museum is an example of a museum entirely dedicated to children. One area is especially designed for children from birth to five, while the rest is for children of all ages. The museum regularly rotates the displays so that they remain appealing to young, inquiring minds. Recent examples included exhibits about spiders, foods, and historic toys. The displays are visually appealing to children, with bright, bold colors. Also, all the displays include hands-on activities to maintain the children's interest, as well as reinforce the concepts.

Another of our local museums, the Arizona Museum of Natural History, contains rare and delicate dinosaur exhibits that cannot be touched. However, the museum offers many interactive displays designed specially for little hands. And there is a kid-friendly room containing toys, books, puzzles, and crafts, all of which relate to the oversized reptiles.

Finally, some museums not designed with younger patrons

in mind still schedule demonstrations, classes, or hands-on activities for children. For example, while both parents and curators at the Phoenix Art Museum would frown upon offering masterpieces as hands-on projects, the museum sponsors the Phoenix Art Kids Days, when youngsters can create their own art.

To save money on museum admission, look for free days or reduced price days. You might also consider purchasing a membership for your favorite museums. As mentioned in the previous section, after a few visits, your membership is paid off. See www.museumspot.com for a listing of museums throughout the United States.

Cultural Arts

Introduce your youngster to the arts by attending plays, symphonies, and concerts. There are few better ways to provide cultural enrichment or foster appreciation for the arts. In addition to the cultural experience, attending performances will help improve attention span and teach appropriate behaviors, such as being quiet and staying seated.

Local theaters and music halls often provide reduced ticket prices during the day or on weeknights. There are even children's theater groups that offer plays such as "The Three Little Pigs" or "Cinderella." If your child is not ready to stay seated for a long time, try outdoor productions held at parks. Performances are often free, sponsored by the city or a production company for the publicity value.

In our community, a local ballet company offered a free performance at the park near our home. Since ballet is not a favorite among many youngsters, including ours, we were able to watch only about one-half of the performance; then we migrated to an open grassy area for a wrestling match between our boys.

Festivities

Local festivals and parades are great fun for the family and can also provide a unique educational opportunity for children. These events expose kids to new foods, cultures, and types of entertainment. At a Renaissance festival, your preschooler can step back in time and learn about the social structure, food, entertainment, dress, occupation, and birds of prey of the Middle Ages. And while your youngster may not be sipping on a draft of Hefeweissen at Oktoberfest, a different German cultural experience will be close at hand. Keep up on various festivals and parades by reading the city newspapers, local Web sites, or parenting magazines. These events are great ways to expose children to a variety of cultures and time periods. Here are a list of festivals, parades, and fairs to inspire your youngster's mind:

- Greek festival
- Oktoberfest
- Irish festival
- Martin Luther King parade
- Veteran's Day parade
- Memorial Day parade
- Fourth of July parade
- St. Patrick's Day parade
- County fair
- State fair

Check out www.festivals.com for more options in your area. Don't forget to include a visit to your county or state fair, which offers diverse educational opportunities from animal shows to science exhibits. You can also get in a ride or two, and grab some cotton candy.

Travel

World travel expands your child's knowledge of geography, history, and different cultures. If you have the means to travel internationally, great. If not, you can still learn a lot visiting neighboring cities or states. America is so culturally diverse and historically rich that in many cities you can experience various cultures in the same afternoon. For example, in Boston, you can walk the Freedom Trail and tour American Revolution sites and later that day visit the Italian district for a pasta dish.

When you travel, try to use a variety of forms of transportation. If you travel across country in a car, you will have a different experience than by air. In a car, you can make stops at your leisure and become more intimately familiar with the region. In this way, you can introduce your youngster to unique animals, architecture, landscape, and people.

On the other hand, traveling by air is an adventure itself. Your preschooler will be fascinated by the trip. The opportunities are endless for learning. How the airplane can get into the air; how the wheels retract; how the airplane lands; and where and how the luggage is stored are just a few of the topics to discuss.

Travel is not in everyone's budget, but dining at your local ethnic restaurant can expose your child to different cultures too. In addition to offering unique foods, many restaurant owners put a great deal of effort into ensuring that the décor introduces patrons to the culture. When you are at a Chinese eatery, not only can your family enjoy a bowl of egg drop soup, but you can point out a statue of Buddha and give your youngster a brief lesson. Or maybe choose a Persian dining experience at another establishment. You can sit on pillows at a low table, while enjoying hummus and kabobs.

Even if you do not leave your house, you can give your

family's taste buds a cultural experience by putting your cooking skills to work at home and creating a foreign dish. Have your child help you with the preparations; you are likely to introduce ingredients that are not common in your everyday fare. No matter how what your "standard" culinary dishes are, don't be afraid to shake it up from time to time.

With the abundance of parenting magazines and newspapers, plus the Internet, it is easier than ever to find out what is happening in your area. The key is to choose an age-appropriate learning activity. Try to schedule field trips at least twice a month for your preschooler. You may even want to invite a few of your son's or daughter's friends along for an extra-special day.

Preschool:

Does My Child Need It?

W E DID NOT ORIGINALLY PLAN to write a chapter on preschool, because the book was intended to help *parents* give their children an intellectual boost by suggesting ideas that parents can use themselves to make their child smarter, independent of whether their kids attend preschool or not. But with so much attention given to early childhood education, we felt it was necessary to address preschool.

For many parents today, sending their children to preschool is a foregone conclusion. But for those who are pondering a different path, the pressure to conform and start their child in a formal preschool program can be overwhelming. *We know*. Before our oldest was two, other parents were asking where we planned to send him to preschool, and the closer he came of age, the more people asked. Like many parents, you may have questions about it all: "Will preschool give my youngster an edge when starting school? Does my child need to attend to be ready to start his or her education? What about socialization? Does he or she need to be in a class with peers to learn how to interact with others?"

Parents must think so; the number of children in preschool has dramatically increased over the last half-century. Between the years 1965 and 2004, preschool enrollment of three-year-olds increased from 4.9 percent to 38.7 percent and from 16.1 percent to 68.4 percent for four-year-olds.[1] In addition to more parents funding their children's preschool education, government programs are more prevalent due to public pressure and demand. Along with federal programs for at-risk children such as Head Start, some states have funded universal preschool.

Why the change? In part because more women are working outside the home. In 1970, 30.8 percent of moms were in the workforce, and by 2000 that number grew to 61.9 percent.[2] As time went on, instead of using daycare, parents placed their children in what they believed was a more beneficial environment—one which would prepare them academically and socially for elementary school. But twice as many working women does not fully explain nearly an eightfold-increase in three-year-olds attending preschool.

Something else is going on: Public perception of the value of preschool has changed.

Preschool Programs

The first research making a substantial impact on both the perception and policy of preschool was the High/Scope Perry Preschool Study in 1962. The study began as an educational intervention for 123 high-risk African-American children with IQs between 70 and 85, which is considered borderline mentally impaired.[3] Fifty-eight children in the treatment group received preschool instruction two and a half hours a week for two years, as well as weekly home visits, and the remaining sixty-five were in the control group. After completion of the study, the children who attended preschool demonstrated cognitive gains. The program appeared a success. Encouraged by the results, in the summer of 1965 President Johnson's administration, as part of the war on poverty, initiated a program called Head Start. The intention was similar to the Perry Preschool Program: to boost the school readiness of low-income children.[4] Children who enrolled were provided a comprehensive battery of services including education; medical, dental, and mental health care; nutrition services; and parental support. Half a million children attended the first eight weeks of the program. The youngsters showed gains across the board—and the organizers were euphoric. But shortly afterwards, the optimism dimmed. As researchers in the Perry Preschool Program were discovering, the cognitive improvements that were so exuberantly trumpeted vanished. The gains "faded out." Since that time, studies have consistently shown that the cognitive gains made during both Head Start and the Perry Preschool Program vanish by the end of grade school.[5]

A third program often cited as evidence that preschool education produces cognitive gains is the Abecedarian Project. According to the researchers, "The Abecedarian Project was designed as an experiment to test the hypothesis that providing socially disadvantaged children with an intellectually stimulating environment from early infancy could prevent the development of mild mental retardation."[6] Like the other programs, the children were from homes that were socially disadvantaged, and the objective of the study was to prevent the onset of mental retardation. This treatment group was different from the middle-class children whose parents today send them to preschool in hopes they will get an intellectual jump start.

The children entered the Abecedarian project during infancy and were provided enriched activities, medical attention, and enhanced nutrition up to age five.[7] The teachers used a curriculum with the infants to develop language, motor, social, and cognitive skills. After age three, the youngsters were exposed to preschool curricula for reading, math, social skills, as well as a pre-phonics reading program. Special emphasis was placed on communication skills; teachers used a language development program and also conversed and read to the kids daily. By the conclusion of the program, the children showed cognitive gains over those in the control group. The program proved children could boost their IQs by attending preschool—or did it?

A closer look at these data leaves one less persuaded. What you notice is this: *All the gains the children in the Abecedarian Program made came prior to age three.*[8] Despite the effort, the children who were provided an enriched preschool experience made no cognitive gains over the control group during the preschool years.

Today it is widely acknowledged among researchers that most preschool programs generate few long-term cognitive gains, and, as a result, the proponents of preschool have reframed the objectives. Rather than boosting intellect, other benefits are cited, such as social, educational, and financial.[9] According to the Office of Juvenile Justice and Delinquency Prevention of the Department of Justice, when those who attended the Perry Preschool Program were compared to the control group, it was found that 14 percent fewer were on welfare; 9 percent fewer had felony arrests; and 17 percent more finished high school.[10] By far the greatest return on investment cited is a somewhat intangible category identified as "savings to crime victims": how much it costs those who are impacted by criminal activity. The distant second are savings on criminal justice costs; for example, the cost of incarceration.

While this may be relevant in a debate on how to help best help those who come from very high-risk environments, the data provides little incentive for the average middle-class family to send their son or daughter to preschool. Do you believe your child will turn to violent crime if he or she does not go to preschool? Or that your child will be on welfare as a result of not attending? Or that perhaps your youngster will not finish high school because he or she was not enrolled? We doubt it.

Moreover, the researchers for the Perry Preschool Study identified the risk factors for delinquency. These factors include: poor attachment to caregivers; poor parenting skills; and multiple family stressors.[11] They also believe, "Early childhood intervention during the preschool years…offers an opportunity to halt the developmental trajectory toward delinquency and related behavioral disorders."[12] In other words, the children were better off because they had been removed from dysfunctional environments. And the more dysfunctional the environment, the more positive the impact an enriched environment will have.

Co-author Renee has worked with convicted juveniles through a court-mandated rehab program, so she has seen first-hand how some children live in a severely deprived environment. On one occasion, she visited one of the children's guardians, who lived in a trailer. She entered the residence to see boxes of cereal stacked on the kitchen table. Upon closer examination, she noticed roaches not only crawling around the cereal boxes, but covering the wall. The guardian turned out to be the child's grandmother, who spoke only limited English and was also responsible for raising several grandchildren on her own. Likewise, in the home of another troubled boy, Renee walked though the front door and saw a baby lying on the concrete floor, staring at the ceiling, surrounded by piles of dirty clothes.

The point we are making in these two cases is that it does not take much improvement to help such children, who have very limited resources and whose parents or guardians probably lack the mindset to provide their youngster with an enriched environment. There will probably be few trips to the zoo, or the museum, or even the library, for that matter. Therefore, any preschool environment would be better than living in such conditions.

Even David Weikart, past president of the Perry Preschool study, agrees that the preschool programs do little for those who do not come from a disadvantaged home. He has said, "For middle-class youngsters with a good economic basis, most programs are not able to show much in the way of difference."[13]

The Effectiveness of Universal Preschool

The research that exists about preschool's effect on children from the middle social economic status (SES) or higher is limited. In general, there is a lack of interest in sponsoring studies that target populations other than at-risk children.

Two studies that did consider kids from varied SES were based upon the universal preschool program through the public schools in Georgia and Oklahoma. The Georgia universal preschool program started in 1993, and the goal was to "provide young children with the learning experiences they need in order to be ready for kindergarten and primary school and to enhance the cognitive and social development of the children."[14] In 1996, the United States Office of School Readiness commissioned a study to determine the effectiveness of the program. Like the other preschool programs, they found "the children's academic, social, and communication skills peaked in first grade and declined through second."[15]

In 1998, a research team from Georgetown University examined children enrolled in the universal preschool program in Tulsa, Oklahoma.[16] The researchers found the children in the program performed better across the board: better on cognitive tests, reading skills, and writing skills, as well as problem-solving. But no long-term observations were conducted. And there is little reason to believe that Oklahoma preschools would be the anomaly, or that the gains made in this program would be sustained.

Why Parents Send Children to Preschool

As we discussed earlier, the increased number of women in the work force has contributed to more children attending preschool. But there are many stay-at-home moms who are enrolling their children in preschool as well. We will now examine the reasons many parents send their children to preschool.

An Intellectual Edge

Many parents send their kids to preschool in the belief that their child will achieve an intellectual edge. But as we have just discussed, the evidence does not support that belief. While such children may surpass their peers initially, there is a little evidence showing long-term cognitive gains. Instead, preschool program research indicates that any cognitive gains are lost in the early elementary years.

Katherine Magnuson from the University of Wisconsin-Madison and a team of researchers observed about 13,000 children and verified the "fade out" phenomenon. The cognitive gains children had made in preschool diminished by elementary school. They found "the positive effects of preschool on academic performance were much reduced by the spring of first grade; we estimate that 60 to 80 percent of the cognitive gains associated with attending preschool and pre-kindergarten had dissipated by that point."[17]

Finally, if preschools are effective in providing a long-term intellectual boost, there should be some improvement in children's test scores due to the increase in preschool attendance. But there isn't. Since the early 1970s, fourth-grade achievement scores have remained stagnant.[18]

So if trained professionals cannot produce long-terms cognitive gains during the preschool years, how can you, the parent, hope to make a difference? *The answer lies within the pages of this book.* The difference comes from talking, playing, and singing with your child. Cognitive gains result from reading together; gardening, cooking, and running errands together; from visiting the library, museum, and zoo. Your child blossoms by participating in a few select classes or sports and playing with friends. And most importantly, success comes from trusting that you, as a parent, can offer all of the intellectual enrichment that your son or daughter needs.

School Readiness

Parents are often concerned that if their youngsters do not first attend preschool, they will not be ready for elementary school; i.e., that they will not be "school-ready." To help address these concerns, the National Education Goals Panel has defined five components, or dimensions, for children to be ready for school.[19] They are:

1. *Physical well-being and motor development*
   A child should have attained age-appropriate physical development and abilities, including fine and gross motor skills. Children should have adequate health care and nutrition when they begin school.
2. *Emotional and social development*
   A child must be emotionally and socially ready to start school. A child's self-image, or perception of himself or herself, affects what he or she attempts. For example, a

child with a more positive self-image will pursue learning more vigorously than a youngster who feels he or she lacks the abilities. Children must be able to express emotions and interpret feelings and know how to share, work with others, and make friends.

3. *Approaches to learning*

"Approaches toward learning" is an umbrella term covering a range of attitudes, habits, and learning styles that are partly genetic, and partly environmental. For example, you have likely found your child demonstrated a certain temperament or disposition right out of the box. This is the genetic aspect, what he or she was born with. On the other hand, as a parent, you do substantially impact your child's curiosity, persistence, personal reflection, imagination, and attention to details. All these factors contribute to how your child thinks and then acts.

4. *Language development*

Language development is critical for memory and analytical skills. The reason people have little memory before age three or four is that they have minimal language skills. As children's language develops, not only are they able to remember events, but they are able to comprehend what someone is saying and communicate with others. Along with verbal skills, children should start school with some early literary skills. The Panel identifies emergent literacy competencies to include:

- Showing interest in literature and recalling stories
- Being aware that the printed word has meaning (phonological awareness)
- Understanding the sequence of stories
- The ability to make primitive symbols, such as an X or a circle

5. *Cognition and general knowledge*
This dimension consists of a general body of knowledge such as knowing letters, numbers, and days of the week. But it also includes comprehension of physical properties of things—that items vary in weight, size, and shape. Children begin to conceive of relationships between different objects. For example, once a child identifies that the cube and sphere are different, the youngster will realize the implication of the differences. As a result of the shape, the ball will roll when pushed, whereas the cube will slide.

Considering these five dimensions, can you determine of your child is ready for school? Not really. Unfortunately, in an effort to be inclusive, the panel did not provide minimum requirements for school readiness. This makes it difficult to assess if your child is in fact "ready" for school. In their policy, the Panel states it "does not believe that there is a single magic threshold above which they [children] are deemed unfit (unready) for school entrance." Furthermore, they report, "The establishment of any single 'readiness' threshold is misleading and dangerous." But one thing you can conclude about preschool is there is nothing on the Panel's list you cannot address at home. Preschool offers nothing magical.

Using data collected by the U.S. Department of Education, Huey-Ling Lin and his colleagues at Alabama State University studied kindergarten teachers' responses when asked what qualities a child should possess to enter school.[20] The teachers identified the abilities to express needs, not be disruptive, follow directions, and take turns as important. In contrast, skills such as knowing the alphabet, colors, or numbers were least important to the teachers. As your authors, we found the results of this survey fascinating. The most important quality identified by the teachers for children to be ready—

emotional maturity—was never proposed as a goal by any of the preschool programs. As we have discussed at length, a stable home environment with enriching activities offers children their best chance for emotional stability.

Likewise, the Child Mental Health Foundations and Agencies Network concluded that in order to be ready to start school, a youngster must be prepared emotionally and socially. They defined readiness characteristics to include confidence, friendliness, and persistence in task completion. Again, contrary to the preschool advocates, the Child Mental Health Foundations and Agencies Network believes these skills are not developed in a preschool environment with other peers. Instead, they begin during the first years of life, with a healthy attachment to a mother or father in a stable home environment.[21]

Socialization

Another reason many moms send their children to preschool is to make sure they get "socialized." Moms often believe acquiring social skills is more important than academic preparation.[22] But in reality, preschools offer few opportunities for social development. Most preschool programs shuffle children from one activity to the next, with little opportunity for the free play that kids need to interact with one another. If lucky, children may have a half an hour a day of free time on the playground.

But children who spend more time with other children in a casual environment have a greater opportunity to improve social skills. The best setting for your child to interact with other youngsters is a weekly playgroup, as we talked about in Chapter 6. Not only do children have more time to interact with their peers, but there is no academic pressure, and parental supervision ensures each child learns to take turns, share, and communicate with other boys and girls. Playgroups can continue for years (as ours has), providing children with a sense of belonging in their early life, and these friendships can be maintained over time.

As we also discussed in Chapter 3, attachment theorists believe the parental relationship determines a child's social skills. In a loving home, a child will develop a sense of self-worth and confidence. This confidence will be apparent when the youngster interacts in a social environment. So, in reality, it can be counterproductive to send a child out with his or her own peers at a young age for the sake of gaining social skills. Instead, the youngster should remain with mom until he or she has a secure attachment; then the child will be prepared to build friendships in a school setting.

Finally, remember children learn to socialize by parental example. Children will copy the behavior they see, both good *and* bad. So keep this in mind when you are in a social environment. Are you polite, thankful, and appreciative with others you come in contact with? Do you try to have a positive attitude through the day? Do you treat others with respect and refrain from gossip? Little eyes are on you, noting every action. You are likely to see a replay of what you say and do months later.

Parents Need Time Alone

We all need time away from our children to get our hair cut, have a cavity filled, shop for a swimsuit, or even drink a cup of coffee and read a magazine. Parents often send their children to preschool to get some time without the kids. No doubt, sending your child into the classroom is one solution, but it is not the only one. Here are some alternatives:

- Share the responsibilities with your spouse by planning ahead. Many professional services offer early morning, late evening, or weekend appointments—utilize these extended hours while one spouse watches the kids.

With a little creativity, you can arrange time without the kids. For example, one spouse can schedule a dentist appointment over the other spouse's lunch hour. The working parent can pick up the kids, have lunch, or go to a nearby park while the other is at the appointment. Of course, every family circumstance is unique, so you will have to see what works best for you.

- If you are fortunate enough to have grandparents or other relatives who live in town, enlist their help. Everyone can win. The children get a break from you and you from the children, and the relatives enjoy spending special time with the children.

- Hire a sitter as needed. There are many sitters available in the daytime hours if you know where to look. Many community college and universities students post for work on bulletin boards. Try the education or psychology department. Students have more flexible hours and are more mature than teenagers. As a bonus, college students are actually studying child development and enjoy working with kids.

- Trade with other parents. If you have a trusted group of moms from your playgroup, neighborhood, or church who have young children, you can take turns watching the kids. The children can play together under the supervision of one mom, while the other goes off on her own. Some playgroups have half of the moms watch the kids, and the other half of the moms can go out child-free. Next time, the roles are reversed.

- Some churches offer a Moms Morning Out. In the church nursery, volunteers or paid staff watch the kids for a few hours while mom does errands. Some churches may also offer daytime Bible Study; the children are cared for in a nearby nursery while moms seek spiritual renewal. A popular Christian support group is Mothers of Preschoolers (MOPS), where moms can get a chance to connect with each other for a few hours while the kids are in the nursery. To find a chapter in your area, go to www.mops.org.

Not Sure What to Do With the Children

Many moms and dads have told us they do not know what to do with their kids. One mom said she felt overwhelmed by her preschool-age children and struggled to keep them busy all day. As parents ourselves, we can empathize. Our advice: Take advantage of the many suggestions in this book to keep your preschooler busy and intellectually enriched.

Parents can make the day more enjoyable for themselves and stimulating for their child by guiding their child from one activity to the next throughout the day. Children prefer structure and, in general, they like consistency. For example, you may have your preschooler play with toys every day after breakfast, then afterward have him or her move on to an art project, or go for a tricycle ride. You need not choreograph the day—your youngster will let you know when to move to the next event. For example, when you see airborne toys in the adjacent room, it is time for a new activity. The key is to keep their minds engaged and thus minimize mischief, while providing enrichment.

In addition to structuring the day, you can also organize the week. You might go to the library every Monday or have playgroup every Friday. As parents, we joke between ourselves that we are under-compensated events coordinators. Make sure, however, you allow time for plenty of unstructured play every single day.

Social Pressure

Coauthor Renee joined a mom's group when our older son was one. When the children in the play group approached the age of three, nearly everyone started making plans for preschool. But as parents, our instinctive response was that preschool was not necessary for everyone. Other moms were surprised to learn we were not planning to send our son. Renee heard such opinions and concerns as, "He won't be socialized," "He won't go to college," "What about learning computers?"; and "How will he handle kindergarten?" from other moms. Many parents simply raised their eyebrows in quiet disapproval.

We have since discovered that many parents send their kids to preschool simply because "everyone else's" kid is going—even if their children have the opportunity to stay home until they are of school age. Since it can be difficult for most people to go against the group consensus—if not impossible for some—in this book we present sound, detailed research and facts about preschool attendance that can help you to resist social pressure.

In the end, we want parents to make an informed decision about whether or not to send to send their child to preschool.

Why *Not* to Send Your Child to Preschool

We opened the chapter by presenting evidence that middle-class children did not show cognitive gains by going to preschool. Then we discussed common reasons parents send their children and provided a rebuttal. Now we will outline the possible detrimental effects preschool can have on children for you to consider before deciding to send your child.

Behavior Problems

Stanford University gathered data from teachers and parents on 14,162 kindergartners through the National Center for Education Statistics to determine the influence of preschool on children. Contrary to the widely held belief that kids need to attend preschool to become better socialized, social development worsened: "We find that attendance in preschool centers, even for short periods of time each week, hinders the rate at which young children develop social skills and display the motivation to engage in classroom tasks, as reported by their kindergarten teachers."[23] The researchers found the youngsters' conduct was worse in three categories: externalizing behaviors, such as aggression, bullying, and acting up; interpersonal skills, such as sharing and cooperation; and problems with self-control in engaging in classroom tasks.

A young child who does not seem ready for the preschool setting may develop behavioral problems. The youngster may act out or lose interest in the school setting, which will plague the child for a lifetime. Rather than place such kids in a formal classroom early in their childhoods, children may do better learning in a relaxed environment at home, in the park, at the zoo, or a museum. These kids also may also do better in shorter one-hour classes than the longer three-hour classes that are typical of preschools. As they mature, these children may experience an increase in their ability to pay attention and do fine when placed in elementary classes.

Labeling Children

Early entry into a formal school setting may be difficult for some young children, especially those who have a more difficult temperament or develop at a slower rate. While some preschool children are ready to sit in a class setting for several hours a day, others lose focus after just a few minutes.

But many teachers have unrealistic expectations for children, which leads to an incorrect diagnosis. In a study we cited in Chapter 7 while discussing television's effect on a child's ability to pay attention, researchers Geist and Young also point out, "Many of ADHD complaints by teachers can be attributed to developmentally inappropriate curriculum for children that ask children to sit quietly and to pay attention for longer periods of time than what could be expected developmentally."[24]

Along with varying attention skills, children have different rates of development. Some children can identify words at age four, while others are still struggling with their letters at the same age. Both kids may be within the wide, normal range of appropriate development. Unfortunately, the children who do not yet match most of their peers' abilities in the classroom may start down a path of academic struggles as a result of being identified as "difficult" or "slow" early on, when in fact they simply are not developmentally ready. Unfortunately for many youngsters, being labeled early may be the beginning of persistent academic problems.

Class Size

According to the National Association for the Education of Young Children (NAEYC), the required minimum teacher-child ratio required for preschool accreditation, depending upon the group size, is one teacher per nine children for three-year-olds and one teacher per ten children for five-year-olds.[25] This means there may be one teacher and one assistant for to up to twenty five-year-old children. But large groups can be overwhelming to some young children. One veteran preschool teacher we know decided not to put her own child in preschool because she saw children frequently withdraw or act out when put into classrooms at an early age.

Rather than starting your child in a large classroom setting, begin with smaller classes and then enroll your youngster in larger classes when he or she is ready. Try the YMCA or the city parks and recreation departments; they often have classes with a few students. (See Chapter 12 for information on these classes.) When your child is three or younger, you might enroll him or her in parent-tot classes, where you can participate with your youngster in class. Your child will have fun in the group setting, but with the security of a parent. At age four, your child will likely be ready for short classes of forty-five minutes to one hour, without parent participation. Make participating in class exciting; tell your child you are anxious to hear all about what the children have done during class. Explain to your child you will be waiting right outside and will be ready to pick him or her up after class has ended. This is a good opportunity for you to have a latte and catch up on a novel. Try one to three short classes a week, depending on your child's interest and temperament. By age five, a two- or three-hour class one day a week, or two or three one-hour classes, without a parent, is usually ideal.

If you introduce your child slowly to larger group classes, by the time a child reaches kindergarten he or she will be comfortable and confident in the classroom. Please remember the ages we suggest are not hard and fast rules, but, as mentioned earlier, may depend upon your child. You must be attuned to your youngster and determine the appropriate age, class size, and duration for your beginning pupil. Some kids might not be ready to participate in a classroom setting until elementary school.

But even when the adjustment to a classroom goes smoothly, personal milestones or achievements at this age are likely to go unnoticed. In preschool, there are too many kids for the teachers to know each child intimately, and they can neither possess nor express the same affection as a parent can. So both you and your child miss out. You are not there to see your child print his or her name for the first time, and your child is not rewarded with a kiss.

Less individual attention can also mean less intellectual stimulation. Young children learn best when help is adjusted to the appropriate level of each individual child.[26] The teacher cannot tailor the assistance for your youngster if there are twenty or more children in the class. And even when there's an assistant, preschoolers still require more individualized attention due to the wide range of developmental abilities.

Barbara Wakik and Mary Bond from Johns Hopkins University studied interactive reading with four-year-old children in a classroom setting. Although the youngsters learned more vocabulary words than their peers in the control group, who did not experience teacher-led reading, the researchers agreed that "classroom experiences cannot possibly match the impact of one-to-one reading"[27] In contrast, learning at home provides the optimum teacher-to-student ratio—one-to-one, or close to it, depending on the size of your family.

Compartmentalization

Parents who send their child to school may inadvertently compartmentalize their child's learning. They may assume all learning has taken place within the classroom and therefore not provide additional learning opportunities at home. Fewer hours are spent reading, playing games, or going to the museum or library. When co-author Renee asked one mother if she planned to take her youngster to the library after the park, she replied, "No. He gets all that at preschool." On the other hand, if you know it is your responsibility to educate your child, you will do so at every available opportunity.

Parental Attachment

As discussed in Chapter 3, children create an attachment with their parents in the first years. If parents hurry to break the attachment before the child is ready, the child may attach to another adult or child. Or a youngster may feel so upset by leaving mom that he or she withdraws and has problems connecting with anyone.

We know a mom who was very anxious to put her child in preschool. When the child was only two and a half years old, she placed her in a highly acclaimed preschool. The child cried every day for three months, but Mom did not respond to her distress. Finally, the child formed a new connection— to the teacher. This was clear when the teacher came to the youngster's birthday party. The child only interacted with the teacher and had very little interest in Mom.

Peer Dependence

Children imitate the attitudes and activities of their peers by the time they reach their preschool years.[28] And as a parent, you know this is not always a good thing. But when your child's social experience is in a play group rather than in a preschool class, you can influence his or her behavior. For example, if your child treats another child inappropriately, you are there to correct the behavior and teach him or her proper social skills. In a preschool situation, on the other hand, where the ratio of kids to teachers is ten to one or so, such improper actions are more likely to go unnoticed.

And while preschool children do attach to their peers, they are better off spending the developmental years with their families. Substantial research suggests children are more independent if formal school is delayed; they tend to be *more* social and display greater leadership.[29]

Cost

The cost of preschools varies from $200 for a month at the local YMCA to more than $1,000 a month for the prestigious "academies" in some cities (as of this writing). Rather than shell out a substantial sum for preschool tuition, we advocate spending your money on museums, music lessons, special interest classes, or educational trips. For all the money you spend on preschool tuition in a year, you can afford a zoo and museum membership, take a weekly music class, and play a different sport every season—and still have money left over.

Variety of Experiences

While saving money by *not* sending your youngster to preschool, you can also introduce your preschooler to a breadth of experiences that he or she would not likely experience in a school setting. One day your child may be at home playing with toys, reading, and doing an art project, while another day he or she might be in a classroom taking a group music class. Likewise, your youngster may spend one afternoon at the park playing with friends and another morning in a museum discovering dinosaurs. Your child may also have more varied social contacts; throughout the week, he or she may interact with peers, grandparents, the baker at the grocery store, his or her coach, and siblings.

Mom May Have More Education

Research has consistently shown that a mother's education level is correlated to a children's cognitive ability.[30] Yet in preschool scenarios, highly educated mothers are often placing their children in the care of those who have fewer school years under their belt. We know one stay-at-home mom who has a graduate degree, yet she pays to send her child to a local university's study lab, where the teachers are rotating university students who are spending time in the preschool to earn credits. Who is teaching whom? It appears the college students have more to gain from the experience than the children in the study lab. So before sending your youngster off, take a look at the credentials of the school's teachers. It is not uncommon for large preschool centers to require only a GED for lead teachers.

Too Much School

The typical American goes to school from kindergarten through twelfth grade. That's thirteen years in school! An additional 15 percent go on to college, and some continue on to graduate school, for a total of nineteen years. So why should we put our youngster in so early, when he or she has so many years of school ahead?

Placing your youngster in preschool can create anxiety for both the parents and children due to the extra time commitments. Most preschools have a minimum of half-day classes three days a week for nine months out of the year. The additional time spent in school can result in more hurried days. And to top it off, as we discussed earlier in the chapter, the research shows preschool does not yield either cognitive or social gains.

On the other hand, if you do not enroll your child in preschool, your schedule is more flexible. You can spend more time with your child and not feel rushed by the rigid time constraints of preschool. And if you decide to take a class or two, the classes you select through community organizations are held for fewer hours a day and might last only six to eight weeks.

What's more, early academics may extinguish a child's desire to learn. Preschool-age children learn best through play and experience, rather than through drills or lectures. A manuscript prepared for the National Educational Goals Panel notes that while early reading drills can improve skills in the short-term, these exercises can also cool youngsters to later reading.[31] Academic-oriented preschool can take the fun out of reading and learning.

No One Cares Like You

No one cares about your things as much as you. No one cares about your money as much as you. No one cares about your car as much as you. No one cares about your home as much as you. Service providers may be professionals and want to do a fine job, but they have little emotional investment in what you have.

The same applies to your child. You care about your youngster the most and put in the greatest effort to shape your child's mind and foster emotional stability. And being the parent, you can show how much you care with hugs and kisses—unlike teachers.

Co-author Renee recently visited a science museum with our two boys. While she was at an exhibit, a group of twenty preschool children and two teachers from an NAEYC-accredited private religious preschool arrived. Most of these kids ran from exhibit to exhibit, randomly pushing buttons and lifting flaps, while Renee was explaining the various types of bugs in one display to our boys. Then a group of five curious students gathered around, trying to listen to her explanations. As Renee and our sons moved to another display, the preschool children followed them, eager to learn more. It was not long before two children started asking Renee questions and tried to get her to come to different exhibits with them. One little boy who was desperate for attention consistently interjected, "Look at this!" or "Come over here!" All this time, the male teacher stood by the door uninterested, while the female teacher sat on a bench toying with her fingernails. When the predetermined time had lapsed, the man bellowed for the children to line up and the woman ushered the children to the next room. Sadly, the parents of these children thought their children had an educational day at the science museum.

This is not an isolated incident. We have frequently encountered preschool children on tours with similarly disinterested teachers. The preschool staff made no attempt whatsoever to engage the children. They were merely facilitators. Can we make a sweeping indictment of all preschools, and all teachers, from our observations? Probably not. But even the most well-meaning and attentive teacher would have a tough time engaging ten preschoolers, or even six for that matter, simultaneously.

Preschooling Without Preschool

If you believe sending your child to preschool is not best for your child or your family, our message is: Don't feel pressured if you do not feel preschool is the right choice. Don't jump on the bandwagon because everyone else is doing it. As we have shown, your child will *not* be at a disadvantage by not attending preschool. In fact, if you create an enriched home environment, your youngster may be better off without it.

Remember, your greatest influence on your child is through playing, talking, and reading. And by following what we have recommended throughout the book, you can provide all the enrichment preschool provides—and more, considering the selection of classes available through the parks and recreation departments, the local YMCA, and music or gymnastic schools. Museums or zoos offer still more opportunities, as previously mentioned. In Phoenix, Arizona, the Desert Botanical Garden has a program for preschoolers called Sammy's Seedlings. Here children meet two hours once a week for eight weeks with a parent for hands-on learning about desert plant and animal life. The Phoenix Zoo offers a program called Farm, Food, and Play, where youngsters and parents do art projects, have interactive stories, share snacks, and learn about animals. Lastly, the Arizona Science Center has Stroller Science classes, where topics vary from solving crimes to an introduction to genetics.

Once again, these are just some examples in our local area. Review prior chapters of our book for more ideas. Then do a little detective work yourself to find what is available in your area. If you live in a rural area, you may not have the same resources available as those in larger cities, so use open spaces for children to learn and explore with your help. It takes additional effort but is time well spent.

If you want to prepare your child for the paper and pencil activities he or she will do in school eventually, there are several things you can do. Encourage your child to write when you do, such as when you are writing a grocery list or paying bills. You can also implement some of our earlier recommendations and use coloring books, sticker books, and arts and crafts projects.

For the older preschooler, you may purchase age-appropriate workbooks. Although they are not mandatory, workbooks can help solidify the learning that has taken place based on the recommendations in this book. Workbooks can be a good way to transition your older preschooler to elementary school. The key to using workbooks successfully is not to push your child before he or she is developmentally ready. You might just do one page a day with your child and make it fun. If your child becomes frustrated, put the book away for another time.

Workbooks for preschool-age children, pre-k, and kindergarten offer colorful pages and interesting characters, which appeal to the young children. Some are designed to cover basic skills required for each age or grade level, while others are topical workbooks that cover phonics, mathematics, mazes, or other subjects. They can be purchased at teaching supply stores, warehouse stores, bookstores, or online at www.amazon.com. Choose them carefully, based on the suggested age recommendations.

Finally, *why rush life?* Our children are only young once. Why not make the most of it by spending as much time as possible with your child? Your youngster should not be the only one to enjoy his or her childhood. So should you.

How to Choose a Preschool

We realize that customizing your child's preschool enrichment is not for everyone. For those families who feel preschool is the best option, there are many choices: private or state-funded (eligibility requirements depend on the state), secular or religious, in a person's home or at an extensive school-only facility. Here are considerations when you make your selection.

Minimal Hours

If your schedule allows, send your child to preschool for a *minimum* number of hours. As we said previously, the most important influence on a child is mom. Long hours in preschool subtract from this precious time. Look for preschool programs that meet two to three times a week for two or three hours a day. Available schedules are typically Monday, Wednesday, and Friday, or Tuesday and Thursday. There are morning and afternoon programs available also, so choose the time that matches your child's temperament.

Although many preschools boast that they provide "all day" care, avoid these. These schools tend to be more daycare centers than places for enriching a preschool child. There is also a greater turnover of staff and children in the larger centers. This is bad for preschoolers, because at this age they need consistent caregivers for appropriate attachment.

Teachers

Consider schools where the staff has good teaching credentials. Look for lead teachers who have a minimum of a bachelor's degree in Early Childhood Education or Elementary Education. Choose preschools where there is a stable staff and the teachers have been there for several years. Don't be afraid to switch teachers or preschools if you feel it is not a good fit for your child. Look for a low student-to-teacher ratio. As we mentioned earlier, the maximum ratio for four-year-olds that NAEYC accreditation allows is ten children per one teacher—but the fewer students per teacher, the better. If you are affiliated with a particular religion, consider a preschool at your church or synagogue. You can be sure that the values taught are in line with you family's.

Preschool Co-op

An alternative to traditional preschool is a cooperative preschool, or co-op. Co-ops provide a professional teaching staff to run the program, while member families share the responsibilities for teaching the children and running the school. Most co-ops are play-oriented and are a good compromise for parents who feel daunted by the task of teaching, yet want to be more involved in their child's education than a traditional preschool allows. Another plus is that the co-op preschool is more affordable, since parents share in the teaching, administration, and maintenance of the school. If a preschool co-op is not available in your area, volunteer in your child's classroom regularly.

Multiage Classes

Some preschools offer classes where children of various ages are grouped together. For preschool-age children, this means placing three- to five-year-olds in the same classroom. As in a play group, the younger children can learn from the older, while the older children can reinforce learned skills by helping the younger ones. You also minimize the competitiveness found when children of the same age are grouped together, because all the youngsters possess different skill levels.

Another benefit is that the children are with the same teacher for two to three years, creating a continuous relationship between teacher and student. The longer relationship maintains consistency for the child and enables the teacher to understand the child's individual development over the entire preschool years.

Play-Oriented Preschool

Louise Miller and Rondeall Bizzell from the University of Louisville studied the long-term effects of Montessori (play-oriented) versus traditional preschool programs.[32] Initially no differences were found, but by second grade those in Montessori scored higher in reading and math achievement, and these differences remained through sixth grade. On the other hand, the children who were in academic schools were more anxious about tests, less creative, and displayed more negative attitudes toward school.

So, when choosing a preschool, look for ones that are play-oriented. Review the school's Web site for the school's philosophy. If it is not clear from the Web site, call the director of the preschool.

Nanny as an Alternative

A mom we know returned to work full-time while her child was still a preschooler. She decided to hire a nanny to care for her. The nanny was carefully screened and was very responsible with the child but was unsure what to do with the youngster every day. We suggested the mother schedule the days for the nanny: choose the classes, playgroup times, and library days. Even game time was planned out. It proved a win/win situation. The nanny felt relieved that she could follow a structured day, the child enjoyed her days more, and the mom was comfortable knowing her daughter was getting the desired attention and enrichment. Also, since mom knew the child's schedule, she could have more engaging conversation with her daughter after work.

Before sending your child to preschool, ask yourself what is to be gained versus what you are giving up. And if you decide preschool is right for your family, make sure you still provide ample time for the many enriching activities we have recommended throughout the book.

Afterword

W
E'VE DISTILLED THE RESULTS of hundreds of studies and provided practical applications, thus giving you the keys to unlock your child's potential. We offer many, many ideas so you can provide your youngster with a more intellectually enriched life. Yet we don't want you to feel overwhelmed or think you need to follow *all* our recommendations. Instead, it is our intention to make parents feel more comfortable by providing good advice backed by the latest solid research about raising their children. We do, however, recommend that you incorporate the fundamentals into your parenting: Be a warm and sensitive parent; verbally engage your child regularly; allow lots of time for free play; and read to him or her daily. Add the extras, such as participating in music and athletics, if it will work for your family.

And while our book focuses on smarter children, the message is to be an involved parent. Your child is your most important investment—and the single greatest contribution you can make is your time. By spending attentive hours with your child, he or she will be not only intellectually stronger, but emotionally sounder as well. Creating a brighter child, as it turns out, is the result of building a strong relationship with your youngster that will prepare him or her for life.

Endnotes

1 Wirt, J., Choy, S., Rooney, P., Provasnik, S., Sen, A., and Tobin, R. (2004). The Condition of Education 2004 (NCES 2004-077). U.S. Department of Education, National Center for Education Statistics. Washington, DC: Government Printing Office.

2 "Georgia Kindergarten Inventory of Developing Skills (GKIDS)," *Office of Standards, Instruction and Assessment.* Retrieved on October 4, 2008, from www.doe. k12.ga.us/ci_testing.aspx; Elissa Gootman, "A Plan to Test the City's Youngest Pupils," *The New York Times,* August 27, 2008.

CHAPTER 1

1 *Webster's Unabridged,* 2nd edition, Random House Reference (New York: Random House, 2001), 990.

2 John W. Santrock, *Life Span Development,* 7th edition (Boston: McGraw Hill Press, 1999), 281.

3 Alfred Binet and Theodore Simon, *The Development of Intelligence in Children* (Nashville: Williams Printing Company, 1980), 9, 37.

4 Ibid., 237–239.

5 Santrock, *Life Span Development,* 11th edition, 331.

6 Ibid.

7 Gale H. Roid and R. Andrew Barram, *Essentials of Stanford-Binet Intelligence Scales (SB5) Assessment,* (New Jersey: Wiley, 2004), 1–2, 9–15.

8 Elizabeth O. Lichtenberger, Alan S. Kaufman, *Essentials of WPPSI-III Assessment* (Hoboken, New Jersey: John Wiley and Sons Inc, 2005), 1, 4–13.

9 Santrock, *Life Span Development,* 11th edition, 333.

10 Howard Gardener, *Intelligence Reframed* (New York: Basic, 1999), 41–43.

11 Gardner, *Intelligence Reframed,* 48–49.

12 Richard J. Herrnstein and Charles Murray, *The Bell Curve* (New York: Simon and Schuster, 1994), 17–19.

13 Herrnstein and Murray, *The Bell Curve,* 22–23, 105–108.

CHAPTER 2

1 Marion Diamond and Janet Hopson, *Magic Trees of the Mind* (New York: Plume Publishing, 1999), 13.
2 Ibid., 31.
3 William T. Greenough, James E. Black, and Christopher S. Wallace, "Experience and Brain Development," *Child Development* 58 (1987), 539–559.
4 Joe L Frost, "Neuroscience, Play, and Child Development" (paper presented at the IPA/USA Triennial National Conference, Longmont, CO, June 18–21, 1998).
5 Lise Eliot, *What's Going On in There?* (New York: Bantam, 1999), 37–38.
6 Diamond and Hopson, *Magic Trees of the Mind*, 58–59.
7 Eliot, *What's Going On in There?* 358–361.
8 Santrock, *Life Span Development*, 11th edition, 163–165.
9 Eliot, *What's Going On In There?* 244–247.
10 Santrock, *Life Span Development*, 7th edition, 131, 201.
11 Santrock, *Life Span Development*, 11th edition, 157–158.
12 Santrock, *Life Span Development*, 11th edition, 256.
13 Santrock, *Life Span Development*, 11th edition, 43–44.
14 Santrock, *Life Span Development*, 11th edition, 178–181.
15 Santrock, *Life Span Development*, 11th edition, 247–250.
16 Mary Ann Spencer Pulaski, *Understanding Piaget: An Introduction to Children's Cognitive Development* (New York: Harper and Row, 1980), 28.
17 Santrock, *Life Span Development*, 11th edition, 247–250.
18 Santrock, *Life Span Development*, 11th edition, 321–322.
19 Santrock, *Life Span Development*, 11th edition, 407–408.

CHAPTER 3

1 Donna K. Ginther and Robert A. Pollack, "Family Structure and Children's Educational Outcomes: Blended Families, Stylized Facts, and Descriptive Regressions," *Demography* 41 (2004), 671–700.
2 Susan S. Lang, "A Grandparent at Home Buffers the Drawbacks of Single-Parenthood, Cornell Study of National Data Finds," *Cornell University News Service* (May 2005), retrieved July 7, 2007 from www.news.cornell.edu/stories/May05/grandparents.kids.ssl.html
3 Santrock, *Life Span Development*, 11th edition, 220–221.
4 John Bowlby, *A Secure Base: Parent Child Attachment and Healthy Human Development* (New York: Basic Books, 1988), 10.
5 Joseph L. Jacobson and Diane E. Wille, "The Influence of Attachmenet Pattern on Developmental Changes in Peer Interaction from the Toddler to the Preschool Period," *Child Devlopment* 57 (1966), 338–347; Kathryn A. Park and Everett Waters, "Security of Attachment and Preschool Friendships," *Child Development* 60 (1989), 1076–1081.
6 Lisa E. Crandell and Peter R. Hobson, "Individual Difference in Young Children's IQ: A Social-Developmental Perspective," *Journal of Child Psychology and Psychiatry* 40 (1999), 455–464.
7 Joanne Roberts, Julie Jurgens, and Margaret Burchinal, "The Role of Home Literacy Practices in Preschool Children's Language and Emergent Literacy Skills," *Journal of Speech, Language, and Hearing Research* 48 (2005), 345–359.
8 Rebecca R. Fewell and Barbara Deutscher, "Contributions of Receptive Vocabu-

lary and Maternal Style: Variables to Later Verbal Ability and Reading in Low-Birthweight Children," (TESCE 22:4 Miami, FL: University of Miami School of Medicine, The Debbie Institute, 2002).

9 Jason T. Downer, and Robert C. Pianta, "Academic and Cognitive Functioning in First-Grade: Associations with Earlier Home and Child Care Predictors and with Concurrent Home and Classroom Experiences," *School Psychology Review* 35 (2006), 11–31.

10 Robert C. Pianta and Katina L. Harbers, "Observing Mother and Child Behavior in a Problem-Solving Situation at School Entry: Relations with Academic Achievement," *Journal of School Psychology* 34 (1996), 307–322.

11 Roberts, Jurgens, and Burchinal, *Journal of Speech, Language, and Hearing Research*, 345–359.

12 Michelle M. Englund, Amy E. Luckner, Gloria L. Whaley, and Byron Egeland, "Children's Achievement in Early Elementary School: Longitudinal Effects of Parental Involvement, Expectations, and Quality of Assistance," *Journal of Educational Psychology* 96 (2004), 723–730.

13 Carol S. Dweck, "Messages That Motivate: How Praise Molds Students' Beliefs, Motivation, and Performance (in Surprising Ways)," *Improving Academic Achievement*, ed. Joshua Aronson (New York: Academic Press, 2002), 37–60.

14 L. S. Vygotsky, *Mind and Society: The Development of Higher Mental Processes* (Cambridge, Massachusetts: Harvard University Press, 1978), 84–91.

15 Lori A. Roggman, Lisa K. Boyce, Gina A. Cook, Katie Christiansen, DeAnn Jones, "Playing with Daddy: Social Toy Play, Early Head Start, and Developmental Outcomes," *Fathering* 2 (2004), 83–108.

16 Petter Kristensen and Tor Bjerkdedal, "Explaining the Relation Between Birth Order and Intelligence," *Science* 316 (2007), 1717.

CHAPTER 1

1 Richard C. Anderson, Elfrieda H. Hiebert, Judith A. Scott, Ian A. G. Wilkinson, "Becoming a Nation of Readers," *The Report of the Commission on Reading* (The National Academy of Education, Washington D.C., 1984).

2 Adriana G. Bus, Marinus G. van Ijzendoorn, and Anthony D. Pellegrini, "Joint Book Reading Makes for Success in Learning to Read: A Meta-Analysis on Intergenerational Transmission of Literacy," *Review of Educational Research* 65 (1995), 1–21.

5 Christopher J. Lonigan, "Conceptualizing Phonological Processing Skills in Prereaders," *Handbook of Early Literacy Research*, Volume 2, ed. David K. Dickinson and Susan B. Neuman (New York: The Guilford Press, 2007), 78.

4 Donald P. Hayes and Margret G. Ahrens, "Vocabulary Simplification for Children: A Special Case of 'Motherese'?" *Child Language* 15 (1988), 395–410.

5 Claudia Robbins and Linnea C. Ehri, "Reading Storybooks to Kindergarteners Helps Them Learn New Vocabulary Words," *Journal of Educational Psychology* 86 (1994), 54–64.

6 Ibid.

7 Ibid.

8 Snow, Catherine E., Porche, Michelle V., and Tabors, Patton O., *Is Literacy Enough?: Pathways to Academic Success for Adolescents* (Baltimore: Paul H. Brooks Publishing Co., Inc., 2007), 20.

9   David K. Dickinson, Allyssa McCabe, Louisa Anastasopoulos, Ellen S. Peisner-Feinberg, and Michele D. Poe, "The Comprehensive Language Approach to Early Literacy: The Interrelationships Among Vocabulary, Phonological Sensitivity, and Print Knowledge Among Preschool-Aged Children," *Journal of Educational Psychology* 95 (2003), 465–481.

10 Ibid.

11 Margaret and H. A. Rey, *Curious George Plays Baseball* (Boston, Houghton Mifflin Company), 1986.

12 Larry Mikulecky, "Family Literacy: Parent and Child Interactions," *Family Literacy: Directions in Research and Implications for Practice* (January 1996): available at www.ed.gov/pubs/FamiLit/parent.html

13 G.J. Whitehurst, F.L. Falco, C.J. Lonigan, J. E. Fischel, D.D. DeBaryshe, M.C. Valdez-Menchaca, and M. Caulfield, "Accelerating Language Development Through Picture Book Reading," *Developmental Psychology* 24 (1988), 552–559.

14 Stan and Jan Berenstain, *The Berenstain Bear Scouts and the Missing Merit Badges* (New York, Scholastic, Inc., 1998).

15 Robbins and Ehri, *Journal of Educational Psychology,* 54–64.

16 Hollis S. Scarborough, Wanda Dobrich, and Maria Hager, "Preschool Literacy Experience and Later Reading Achievement," *Journal of Learning Disabilities* 24 (1991), 508–511.

17 Richard Scarry, *Best Word Book Ever* (New York: Golden Books, 1999), 18–19.

18 Dickinson, McCabe, Anastasopoulos, Peisner-Feinberg, and Poe, *Journal of Educational Psychology*, 465–481.

19 Donald S. Hayes, "Young Children's Phonological Sensitivity After Exposure to a Rhyming or NonRhyming Story," *Journal of Genetic Psychology* 162 (2001), 253–260.

20 P.E. Bryant, M. MacLean, L.L. Bradley, and J. Crossland, "Rhyme and Alliteration, Phoneme, Detection, and Learning to Read," *Developmental Psychology* 26 (1990), 429–438.

21 Catherine Snow, "Literacy and Language: Relationships During the Preschool Years," *Harvard Educational Review* 53 (1983), 165–189.

22 Dr. Seuss, *There's a Wocket in my Pocket* (New York: Random House, 1974).

23 Robbins and Ehri, *Journal of Educational Psychology,* 54–64.

24 Jacob W. Grimm and Wilhelm Karl Grimm, *Grimm's Complete Fairy Tales* (Garden City, NJ: Double Day Books, 1990), 81.

25 Patricia Greenfield, Dorathea Farrar, and Jessica Beagles-Roos, "Is the Medium the Message?: An Experimental Comparison of the Effects of Radio and Television on Imagination," *Journal of Applied Developmental Psychology* 7 (1986), 201–218.

26 Beth Casey, Joanne E. Kersh, and Jessica Mercer Young, "Storytelling Sagas: An Effective Medium for Teaching Early Childhood Mathematics," *Early Childhood Research Quarterly* 19 (2004), 167–172.

27 Stuart Murphy, *The Best Bug Parade* (New York: Harper Collins, 1996).

28 Grace Maccarone, *The Silly Story of Goldilocks and the Three Squares* (New York: Cartwell Books, 1996).

CHAPTER 5

1   Santrock, *Life Span Development*, 11th edition, 194, 261.

2   Santrock, *Life Span Development*, 11th edition, 260–262.

3 Santrock, *Life Span Development*, 11th edition, 260.

4 Barbara Tizard, Oliver Cooperman, Anne Joseph, and Jack Tizard, "Environmental Effects on Language Development: A Study of Young Children in Long-Stay Residential Nurseries," *Child Development* 43 (1972), 337–358.

5 Andrew Biemiller, "Vocabulary: Needed if More Children Are to Read Well," *Reading Psychology* 24 (2003), 323–335.

6 Elaine Reese, "Predicting Children's Literacy fro Mother-Child Conversations," *Cognitive Development* 10 (1995), 381–405.

7 Robyn Fivush, Catherine A. Haden, and Elaine Reese, "Elaborating on Elaborations: Role of Maternal Reminiscing Style in Cognitive and Socioemotional Development," *Child Development* 77 (2006), 1568–1588.

8 NICHD Early Child Care Research Network, "Pathways to Reading. The Role of Oral Language in the Transition to Reading," *Developmental Psychology* 41 (2005), 428–442.

9 Snow, Porche, and Tabors, *Is Literacy Enough?: Pathways to Academic Success for Adolescents*, 16.

10 Susan H. Landry, and Karen E. Smith, "The Influence of Parenting on Emerging Literacy Skills," *Handbook of Early Literacy Research*, 135–148.

11 Diamond and Hopson, *Magic Trees of the Mind*, 179–180.

12 Prentice Starkey, Alice Klein, and Ann Wakeley, "Enhancing Young Children's Mathematical Knowledge Through a Pre-Kindergarten Mathematics Intervention," *Early Childhood Research Quarterly* 19 (2004), 99–120.

13 Andrea Mechelli, Jenny T. Crinion, Uta Noppeney, John O'Doherty, John Ashburner, Richard S. Frackowiak, and Cathy J. Price, "Neurolinguistics: Structural Plasticity in the Bilingual Brain," *Nature* 431 (2004), 757.

14 William Derrick, "An Early Language Immersion Model in a Demonstration," *ADFL Bulletin* 10 (1978), 34–36.

15 Penelope W. Armstrong and Jerry D. Rogers, "Basic Skills Revisited: The Effects of Foreign Language Instruction on Reading, Math and Language Arts," *Learning Languages* 2 (1997), 20–31.

16 Marie T. Banich, *Neuropsychology* (New York: Houghton Mifflin, 1997), 474.

17 Derrick, *ADFL Bulletin*, 34–36.

18 Patricia K. Kuhl, Feng-Ming Tsao, and Huei-Mei Liu, "Foreign-language Experience in Infancy: Effects of Short-Term Exposure and Social Interaction on Phonetic Learning," *PNAS* 100 (2003), 9096–9101.

CHAPTER 6

1 Stephen DePaul, "Phenomenological Criticism," *Encyclopedia of Contemporary Literary Theory: Approaches, Scholars, Terms* ed. Irena B. Makaryk (Toronto: University of Toronto Press, 1993), 145.

2 Mehri Takhvar, "Play and Theories of Play: A Review of the Literature," *Early Child Development and Care* 39 (1988), 221–224.

3 Rheta DeVries, "Transforming the "Play-Oriented Curriculum," and Work in Constructivist Early Education," *Children in Play, Story, and School* ed. Artin Goncu and Elsia L. Klien (New York: The Guilford Press, 2001), 74.

4 Doris Bergen, "Stages of Play and Development," *Play as a Medium for Learning and Development: A Handbook of Theory and Practice* ed. Doris Bergen (Portsmouth: Heinemann, 1988), 50.

5   Irene Athey, "The Relationship of Play to Cognitive, Language, and Moral Development," *Play as a Medium for Learning and Development: A Handbook of Theory and Practice*, 87.

6   Anna Bondioli, "The Adult as a Tutor in Fostering Children's Symbolic Play," *Children in Play, Story, and School*, 108.

7   A. D. Pellegrini, "The Relationship Between Kindergartener's Play and Achievement in Prereading, Language, and Writing," *Psychology in the Schools* 17 (1980), 530–535.

8   Shirley R. Wyver and Susan H. Spence, "Play and Divergent Solving: Evidence Supporting a Reciprocal Relationship," *Early Education and Development* 10 (1999), 419–444.

9   Sandra W. Russ, Andrew L. Robins, and Beth A. Christiano, "Pretend Play: Longitudinal Prediction of Creativity and Affect in Fantasy in Children," *Creativity Research Journal* 12 (1999), 129–139.

10 Eli Saltz, David Dixon, and James Johnson, "Training Disadvantaged Preschoolers on Various Fantasy Activities: Effects on Cognitive Functioning and Impulse Control," *Child Development* 48 (1977), 367–380.

11 Thomas Daniels Yawkey, "Sociodramatic Play Effects on Mathematical Learning and Adult Ratings of Playfulness in Five Year Olds," *Journal of Research and Development in Education* 14 (1981), 30–39.

12 Helga Andresen, "Role Play and Language Development in the Preschool Years," *Culture and Psychology* 11 (2005), 387–414.

13 Pellegrini, *Psychology in the Schools*, 530–535.

14 Peter K. Smith and Susan Dutton, "Play and Training in Direct and Innovative Problem Solving," *Child Development* 50 (1979), 830–836.

15 Charles Wolfgang, Laura Stannard, and Ithel Jones, "Advanced Constructional Play with Legos Among Preschoolers as a Predictor of Later School Achievement in Mathematics," *Early Child Development and Care* 173 (2003), 467–475.

16 Artin Goncu and Suzanne Gaskins, "Play and Development: Evolutionary, Sociocultural, and Functional Perspectives," *Play as a Medium for Learning and Development: A Handbook of Theory and Practice*, 106.

17 Danette Glassy, Judith Romano, and Committee on Early Childhood, Adoption, and Dependent Care, "Selecting Appropriate Toys for Young Children: The Pediatrician's Role," *Pediatrics* 111 (2003), 911–913.

18 Kenneth R. Ginsburg, The Committee on Communications, and The Committee on Psychosocial Aspects of Child and Family Health, "The Importance of Play in Promoting Healthy Child Development and Maintaining Strong Parent-Child Bonds," *Pediatrics* 119 (2007), 182–191.

19 Greta G. Fein, "Pretend Play in Childhood: An Integrative Review," *Child Development* 52 (1981), 1095–1118.

20 Tracy R. Gleason , Anne M. Sebanc, and Willard W. Hartup, "Imaginary Companions of Preschool Children," Developmental Psychology 36 (2000), 419–428.

21 Paige C. Pullen and Laura M. Justice, "Enhancing Phonological Awareness, Print Awareness, and Oral Language Skills in Preschool Children," *Intervention in School and Clinic* 39 (2003), 97–98.

22 Diamond and Hopson, *Magic Trees of the Mind*, 201.

23 Stephen R. Burgess, "The Development of Phonological Sensitivity," *Handbook of Early Literacy Research*, 91–93.

24 Gary W. Ladd and Beckie S. Golter, "Parents' Management of Preschooler's Peer Relations: Is it Related to Children's Social Competence?" *Developmental Psychology* 24 (1988), 109–117.

25 Ginsburg, The Committee on Communications, and The Committee on Psychosocial Aspects of Child and Family Health, *Pediatrics*, 182–191.

26 Goncu and Gaskins, *Play as a Medium for Learning and Development: A Handbook of Theory and Practice*, 106.

27 Ginsburg, The Committee on Communications, and The Committee on Psychosocial Aspects of Child and Family Health, *Pediatrics*, 182–191.

CHAPTER 7

1 Victoria J. Rideout, Elizabeth A. Vandewater, and Ellen A. Wartella, "Zero to Six: Electronic Media in the Lives of Infants, Toddlers, and Preschoolers, *The Henry J. Kaiser Family Foundation,* Fall 2003, Menlo Park, CA, available at www.kff.org

2 Dish Network—America's Everything Pack, retrieved May 5, 2007 from www.dishnetwork.com

3 Rideout, Vandewater, and Wartella, *The Henry J. Kaiser Family Foundation*

4 Frederick J. Zimmerman, and Dimitri A. Chrisitakis, "Children's Television Viewing and Cognitive Outcomes," *Archives of Pediatric and Adolescent Medicine* 159 (2005), 619–625; Rideout, Vandewater, and Wartella, *The Henry J. Kaiser Family Foundation.*

5 Federal Communications Commission, *Policies and Rules Concerning Children's Television Programming,* MM Docket No. 93-48 FCC 96-335 (August 8, 1996), Washington, D.C., available at http://www.fcc.gov/Bureaus/Mass_Media/Orders/1996/fcc96335.htm

6 Ibid.

7 Ibid.

8 Shalom M. Fisch and Rosemarie T. Truglio, "Introduction," *"G" is for Growing: Thirty Years of Research on Children and Sesame Street,* ed. Shalom M. Fisch and Rosemarie T. Truglio (Mahwah, NJ: Lawrence Erlbaum Associates, 2001), xvi.

9 Edward L. Palmer and Shalom M. Fisch, "The Beginnings of Sesame Street Research," *"G" is for Growing,* 5.

10 Ibid., 6–7.

11 Gerald S. Lesser and Joel Schneider, "Creation and Evolution of the Sesame Street Curriculum," *"G" is for Growing,* 31.

12 John C. Wright, Aletha C. Huston, Ronda Scantlin, and Jennifer Kolter, "Creation and Evolution of the Sesame Street Curriculum," *"G" is for Growing,* 108–111; Mabel L. Rice, Aletha C. Huston, and Rosemarie Truglio, "Words from 'Sesame Street': Learning Vocabulary While Viewing," *Developmental Psychology* 26 (1990), 421–428; Rupin R. Thakkar, Michelle M. Garrison, and Dimitri A. Christakis, "A Systematic Review for the Effects of Television Viewing by Infants and Preschoolers," *Pediatrics* 118 (2006), 2025–2031.

13 Daniel R. Anderson, Aletha C. Huston, Kelly L. Schmitt, Deborah L. Linebarger, and John C. Wright, "Early Childhood Television Viewing and Adolescent Behavior: The Recontact Study," *Monograph of Social Research and Child Development* 66 (2001), 1–147.

14 Linda M. Espinosa, James M. Laffery, Tiffany Whittaker, and Yanyan Sheng, "Technology in the Home and the Achievement of Young Children: Findings

From the Childhood Longitudinal Study," *Early Education and Development* 17 (2006), 421–441.

15 Thakkar, Garrison, and Christakis, *Pediatrics* 118: 2025–2031.

16 Greenfield, Farrar, and Beagles-Roos, *Journal of Applied Developmental Psychology*, 201–218.

17 Dimitri A. Christakis and Frederick J. Zimmerman, "Early Television Viewing Is Associated with Protesting Turning Off the Television at Age 6," *Medscape General Medicine* 8 (2006), 63, available at http://www.medscape.com/viewarticle/531503

18 Ibid.

19 Anderson, Huston, Schmitt, Linebarger, and Wright, *Monograph of Social Research and Child Development*, 1–147.

20 Shalom M Fisch and Rosemarie T. Truglio, *"G" is for Growing*, 75–77.

21 Dimitri A. Christakis, Frederick J. Zimmerman, David L. DiGiuseppe, and Carolyn A. McCarty, "Early Television Exposure and Subsequent Attentional Problems in Children," *Pediatrics* 113 (2004), 708–713.

22 Eugene A. Geist and Marty Gibson, "The Effect of Network and Public Television Programs on Four and Five Year Olds' Ability to Attend to Educational Tasks," *Journal of Instructional Psychology,* 27 (2000), 250–261.

23 Carl Erik Landhuis, Richie Poulton, Robert John Hancox, "Does Childhood Television Viewing Lead to Attention Problems in Adolescence? Results From a Prostpective Longitudinal Study," *Pediatrics* 120 (2007), 532–537.

24 Nary Shin, "Exploring Pathways From Television Viewing to Academic Achievement in School Age Children," *Journal of Genetic Psychology* (2004), 367–381.

25 Rideout, Vandewater, and Wartella, *The Henry J. Kaiser Family Foundation.*

26 Robert J. Hancox, Barry J. Milne, and Richie Poulton, "Association of Television Viewing During Childhood With Poor Educational Achievement," *Archives of Pediatric Adolescent Medicine* 159 (2005), 614–618.

27 Angela Teresa Clarke and Beth Kutz-Costes, "Television Viewing, Educational Quality of the Home Environment, and School Readiness," *Journal of Educational Research* 90 (1997), 279–285.

28 Elizabeth A. Vandewater, David S. Bickham, and June H. Lee, "Time Well Spent? Relating Television Use to Children's Free-Time Activities," *Pediatrics* 117 (2006), e181–e191.

29 Committee on Public Education, "American Academy of Pediatrics: Children, Adolescents, and Television," *Pediatrics* 107 (2001), 423–426.

30 Douglas A. Gentile and David A. Walsh, "A Normative Study of Family Media Habits," *Applied Developmental Psychology* 23 (2002), 157–178.

31 Douglas A. Gentile, Charles Oberg, Nancy E. Sherwood, Mary Story, David A. Walsh, and Marjorie Hogan, "Well-Child Visits in the Video Age: Pediatricians and the American Academy of Pediatrics' Guidelines for Children's Media Use," *Pediatrics* 114 (2004), 1235–1241.

32 Xiaoming Li and Melissa S. Atkins, "Early Childhood Computer Experience and Cognitive and Motor Development," *Pediatrics* 113 (2004), 1715–1722.

33 Rosalyn Shute and John Miksad, "Computer Assisted Instruction and Cognitive Development," *Child Study Journal* 27 (1997), 237–254.

34 Feng S. Din and Josephine Calao, "The Effects of Playing Educational Video Games on Kindergarten Achievement," *Child Study Journal* 31 (2001), 95–102

35 Espinosa, Laffey, Whittaker, Sheng, *Early Education and Development*, 421–441.
36 P. S. Klein, O. Nir-Gal and E. Darom, "The Use of Computers in Kindergarten, with or without Adult Mediation; Effects on Children's Cognitive Performance and Behavior," *Computers in Human Behavior* 16 (2000), 591–608.
37 Shute and Miksad, *Child Study Journal*, 237–254.
38 Ibid.
39 Ibid.
40 P. S. Klein, O. Nir-Gal and E. Darom, *Computers in Human Behavior*, 591–608.
41 Xiaoming Li, Melissa S. Atkins, and Bonita Stanton, "Effects of Home and School Computer Use on School Readiness and Cognitive Development Among Head Start Children: A Randomized Control Pilot Trial," *Merrill-Palmer Quarterly* 52 (2006), 239–263.
42 Shute and Miksad, *Child Study Journal*, 237–254.
43 Carol Tell, "The I-Generation—From Toddlers to Teenagers: A Conversation with Jane M. Healy," *Educational Leadership* (October, 2000), 8–13.
44 Entertainment Software Ratings Board, available at www.esrb.org/ratings/ratings_guide.jsp
45 David A. Walsh and Douglas A. Gentile, "A Validity Test of Movie, Television, and Video-Game Ratings," *Pediatrics* 107 (2001), 1302–1308.
46 Gentile and Walsh, *Applied Developmental Psychology*, 157–178.

CHAPTER 8

1 Gordon L. Shaw, *Keeping Mozart in Mind* (San Diego: Elsevier Academic Press, 2004), 6.
2 Frances H. Rauscher, Gordon L. Shaw, and Katherine N. Ky, "Music and Spatial Task Performance," *Nature* 365 (1993), 611.
3 Frances H. Raucher and Gordon L. Shaw, "Key Components of the Mozart Effect," *Perceptual and Motor Skills* 86 (1998), 835–841.
4 Lois Hetland, "Listening to Music Enhances Spatial-Temporal Reasoning: Evidence for the 'Mozart Effect,'" *Journal of Aesthetic Education* 34 (2000), 105–148.
5 Ibid.
6 Frances H. Rauscher, Gordon L. Shaw, Linda J. Levine, Eric L. Wright, Wendy R. Dennis, and Robert L. Newcomb, "Music Training Causes Long-Term Enhancement of Preschool Children's Spatial-Temporal Reasoning," *Neurological Research* 19 (1997), 2–8.
7 Frances H. Rauscher and Mary Anne Zupan, "Classroom Keyboard Instruction Improves Kindergarten Children's Spatial-Temporal Performance," *Early Childhood Research Quarterly* 15 (2000), 215–228.
8 Lois Hetland, "Learning to Make Music Enhances Spatial Reasoning," *Journal of Aesthetic Education* 34 (2000), 179–219.
9 Kathryn Vaughn, "Music and Mathematics: Modest Support for the Oft-Claimed Relationship," *Journal of Aesthetic Education* 34 (2000), 149–166.
10 Sima H. Anvari, Laurel J. Trainor, Jennifer Woodside, and Betty Ann Levy, "Relations Among Musical Skills, Phonological Processing, and Early Reading Ability in Preschool Children," *Journal of Experimental Child Psychology* 83 (2002), 111–130.
11 Joyce Eastlund Gromko, "The Effect of Music Instruction on Phonemic Aware-

ness in Beginning Readers," *Journal of Research in Music Education* 53 (2005), 199–209.

12 Irving Hurwitz, Peter H. Wolff, Barrie D. Bortnick, and Klara Kokas, "Nonmusical Effects of the Kodaly Music Curriculum in Primary Grade Children," *Journal of Learning Disabilities* 8 (1975), 45–174.

13 Susannah J. Lamb and Andrew H. Gregory, "The Relationship Between Music and Reading in Beginning Readers," *Educational Psychology* 13 (1993), 19–28.

14 Robert J. Zatorre, "Absolute Pitch: A Model for Understanding the Influence of Genes and Development," *Nature Neuroscience* 6 (2003), 692–695.

15 Kenneth K. Guilmartin and Lili M. Levinowitz, *Music and Your Child: A Guide for Parents and Caregivers* (Princeton: Music Together Center for Music and Young Children, 2003), 24–31.

16 Terry D. Bilhartz, Rick A. Bruhn, and Judith Olsen, "The Effect of Early Music Training on Child Cognitive Development," *Journal of Applied Developmental Psychology* 20 (1999), 615–636.

17 Hetland, *Journal of Aesthetic Education*, 179–219.

18 Ibid.

CHAPTER 9

1 Gentile and Walsh, *Applied Developmental Psychology*, 157–178.

2 "The Importance of Family Dinners II," *The National Center on Addiction and Substance Abuse at Columbia University* (New York: 2005), www.casacolumbia.org

CHAPTER 11

1 "The Role of Media in Childhood Obesity," *The Henry J. Kaiser Family Foundation,* February 2003, Menlo Park, CA, available at www.kff.org

2 Jianghong Liu, Adrian Raine, Peter H. Venables, Cyril Dalais, and Sarnoff A. Mednick, "Malnutrition at Age 3 Years and Lower Cognitive Ability at Age 11 Years," *Archives of Pediatrics and Adolescent Medicine* 157 (2003), 593–600.

3 U.S. Department of Agriculture, *The Food Pyramid Guide for Young Children* (1999). Retrieved on February 12, 2006, from www.cnpp.usda.gov

4 Jeff Victoroff, *Saving Your Brain* (New York: Bantam Dell, 2002), 229.

5 "Exercise Makes Mice Smarter, Salk Scientists Demonstrate," *The Salk Institute for Biological Studies*, November 1999, La Jolla, CA, available at www.salk.edu

CHAPTER 13

1 "Digest of Education Statistics: 2005," *National Center for Education Statistics.* Retrieved on July 27, 2007, from http:nces.ed.gov/programs/digest/d05/tables/dt05_040.asp

2 Charles Bruner, Sheri Floyd, and Abby Copeman, "Seven Things Policy Makers Need to Know About School Readiness," *State Early Childhood Policy Technical Assistance Network* (Des Moines, IA, January 2005), available at www.cfpciowa.org

3 Greg Parks, "The High/Scope Perry Preschool Project," *Juvenile Justice Bulletin* (October 2000), retrieved on August 3, 2007, from http://ncjrs.gov/html/ojjdp/2000_10_1/contents.html

4 Westat, "Head Start Impact Study," *Head Start Research* (June 2005), U.S. Department of Health and Human Services: Washington, D.C.

5 Herrnstein and Murray, *The Bell Curve*, 403–405.

6 Craig T. Ramey and Frances A. Campbell, "Preventive Education for High-Risk Children: Cognitive Consequences of the Carolina Abecedarian Project," *American Journal of Mental Deficiency* 89 (1984), 515–523.

7 Ibid.

8 Frances A. Campell and Craig T. Campbell, "Effects of Early Intervention on Intellectual and Academic Achievement: A Follow-Up Study of Children from Low-Income Families," *Child Development* 65 (1994), 684–698.

9 Schweinhart, Lawrence J. "The High/Scope Perry Preschool Study Through Age 40: Summary, Conclusions, and Frequently Asked Questions." (Monographs of the High/Scope Educational Research Foundation, 8, 1998), Ypsilanti, MI: High/Scope Press, in press.

10 Parks, *Juvenile Justice Bulletin*

11 Ibid.

12 Ibid.

13 Kenneth T. Walsh, Betsy Streisand, Carolyn Kleiner, and Joe Holley, "The Three Rs and the Big P," *U.S. News and World Report* 127 (1999), retrieved on January 13, 2007, from http://www.usnews.com/usnews/news/articles/990830/archive_001731.htm

14 Gary T. Henry, Craig S. Gordon, Laura W. Henderson, and Bentley D. Ponder, "Georgia Pre-K Longitudinal Study: Final Report 1996–2001," retrieved on January 13, 2007, from http://aysps.gsu.edu/publications/GPKLSFinalReportMay2003.pdf

15 Ibid.

16 William T. Gromley Jr., Ted Gayer, Deborah Phillips, and Brittany Dawson, "The Effects of Universal Pre-K on Cognitive Development," *Developmental Psychology* 41 (2005), 872–884.

17 Katherine Magnuson, Marcia K. Meyers, Christopher J. Ruhm, and Jane Waldfogel, "Inequality in Children's School Readiness and Public Funding," *Focus* 24 (2005), 12–18.

18 Darcy Olsen and Lisa Snell, "Assessing Proposals for Preschool and Kindergarten: Essential Information for Parents, Taxpayers and Policymakers," *Reason Public Policy Institute* (Los Angeles, 2006), at www.reason.org

19 Sharon Lynn Kagan, "Reconsidering Children's Early Development and Learning: Toward Common Views and Vocabulary," *National Education Goals Panel* (Washington, DC: U.S Government Printing Office, 1995), retrieved on June 24, 2007, from http://eric.ed.gov/ERICDocs/data/ericdocs2sql/content_storage_01/0000019b/80/14/5c/d3.pdf

20 Huey-Ling Lin, Frank R. Lawrence, and Jeffrey Gorrell, "Kindergarten Teachers' Views of Children's Readiness for School," *Early Childhood Research Quarterly* 18 (2003), 225–237.

21 Child Mental Health Foundations and Agencies Network, "A Good Beginning: Sending America's Children to School with the Social and Emotional Competence They Need to Succeed." (Monographs of the National Institute of Mental Health). Bethesda, MD: Office of Communications and Public Liaison, available at www.nimh.nih.gov/childhp/fdnconsb.htm

22 Janice Kennedy, "Relationship of Maternal Beliefs and Childrearing Strategies to Social Competence in Preschool," *Child Study Journal* 22 (1992), 39–61.

23 Susanna Loeb, Margaret Bridges, Daphna Bassok, Bruce Fuller, and Russ Rum-
berger, "How Much is Too Much? The Influence of Preschool Centers on Children's Development Nationwide." (Paper presented at the Association for Policy
Analysis and Management, Washington, D.C. November 4, 2005).

24 Geist and Gibson, *Journal of Instructional Psychology*, 250–261.

25 NAEYC Accreditation Criteria, "Teacher-Child Ratios Within Group Size," *National Association for the Education of Young Children* (2005), retrieved July 22,
2007, from www.naeyc.org/academy/criteria/teacher_child_ratios.html

26 Catherine Snow, "Literacy and Language: Relationships During the Preschool
Years," *Harvard Educational Review* 53 (1983), 165–189.

27 Barbara A. Wasik and Mary Alice Bond, "Beyond the Pages: Interactive Book Reading and Language Development in Preschool Classrooms," *Journal of Educational
Psychology* 93 (2001), 243–250.

28 Raymond S. Moore and Dorothy N. Moore, *School Can Wait* (Provo: Brigham
Young University Press, 1979), 55.

29 Moore and Moore, *School Can Wait*, 56.

30 Downer and Pianta, *School Psychology Review*, 11–31

31 Kagan, *National Education Goals Panel*.

32 Louise B. Miller and Rondeall P. Bizzell, "Long-Term Effects of Four Preschool
Programs: Sixth, Seventh, and Eighth Grades," *Child Development* 54 (1983),
727–741.

Index

To order copies of this book
and for product recommendations
visit **www.BrighterInsights.com**